Ed Edwards

ENGLAND
— & SON —

An abridged version of *England & Son* premiered at
Paines Plough's Roundabout at Summerhall,
Edinburgh Festival Fringe on 2nd August 2023 before
embarking on a national tour from September 2023

ENGLAND
— & SON —
by Ed Edwards

The company for the Edinburgh Fringe 2023 production of
England & Son were:

Performer	Mark Thomas
Writer	Ed Edwards
Director	Cressida Brown
Lighting Designer	Richard Williamson
Sound Designer	Michael John McCarthy
Movement Director	Simon Jones
Movement Consultant	Kate Sagovsky
Production Stage Manager	Tine Selby

MARK THOMAS – PERFORMER

Mark Thomas has been a performer for 37 years; in his career he has had a TV show that changed the law, exposed corporate wrongdoing and put gun runners in jail. He has written plays, books and radio shows. He has awards ranging from four Fringe Firsts to a UN Association Global Human Rights Defender Award. This is the first play written for him.
www.markthomasinfo.co.uk

ED EDWARDS – WRITER

Ed wrote and had published his first two novels while serving a three-and-a-half-year prison sentence for drug offences. Many years clean now, Ed went on to write for TV and Radio, as well as writing short films for BBC 2 and Channel 4.

His most recent stage play, *The Political History of Smack and Crack*, won a Lustrum Award at the Edinburgh Fringe, toured nationally and is currently in pre-production as an animated feature film.

Ed is co-artistic director (with fellow writer and actor Eve Steele) of Most Wanted, a theatre and film production company based in Manchester, which concentrates on work grounded in their joint lived experience of addiction and crime. Through Most Wanted, Ed directed Eve Steele's hit theatre show *Life By The Throat* and co-directed the feature film *Scrambled*, currently in post-production.

Ed also teaches creative writing at a small northern university and is currently making a series of narrative films with addicts in treatment for a Lancashire substance misuse and mental health charity.
www.mostwantedshows.com

CRESSIDA BROWN – DIRECTOR

Cress directed Ed Edward's award-winning *The Political History of Smack and Crack* at Paines Plough's Roundabout, Soho Theatre and UK tour.

She was resident director at the National Theatre Studio from 2007 – 2008 and has extensively directed classical work nationally and internationally - including for the Globe, RSC and British Council. These productions have included a *Twelfth Night* performed in Mandarin, a *Cinderella* in Georgian, and Moliere's *Le Malade Imaginaire* in French.

She is probably best known for: *Amphibians* by Steve Waters, inspired from interviews with former Olympic swimmers and staged in the hidden pool under the Bridewell Theatre stage; the collection of plays *Walking the Tightrope* by writers including Caryl Churchill, Timberlake Wertenbaker and Gbolahan Obisesan about freedom of expression; and the UK premiere of *Caught* by Obie Award winner Chris Chen.

After nearly twenty years of directing, Cress is probably most proud of *Septimus Bean and His Amazing Machine* by Adam Peck where she transformed the Unicorn Theatre foyer into a playground for her six-year-old audience during the final scene.

RICHARD WILLIAMSON – LIGHTING DESIGNER

Previous work includes: The Olivier award-winning *Rotterdam* (West End/Off-Broadway/UK National Tour); *Dogs of Europe* (Belarus Free Theatre at the Barbican and international tour); *Richard III, An Arab Tragedy* (Swan Theatre Stratford/International tour); *Sampled and Danse Élargie* (Sadler's Wells); *Great Expectations* (UK tour); *Fiddler on the Roof* (Cemil Topulzu Open-Air Theatre); *Beowulf, Septimus Bean and His Amazing Machine, Jason and the Argonauts* (Unicorn); What's On Stage 'Best Production' Winner *Thebes Land* (also video); *New Nigerians, Drones Baby Drones* (also video); *Shrapnel* (also video); *Mare Rider* (Arcola Theatre); *The Political History of Smack and Crack* (Edinburgh Fringe and Soho Theatre); *Oedipus at Colonus* (Cambridge Arts Theatre); *The Body* (Barbican); *The Dark Side of Love* (Roundhouse); *Amphibians* (Bridewell); *Thrill Me* (UK and international tour); *Twentieth Century Boy* (New Wolsey Ipswich); *Re:Home* (also video); *Brenda* (The Yard); *The Al-Hamlet Summit* (Tokyo International Festival/International tour).

Richard trained at LAMDA, is a Trustee of the Kings Head Theatre, and develops industry leading applications zoomOSC and zoomISO.

www.richard-williamson.com

MICHAEL JOHN McCARTHY – SOUND DESIGNER

Michael John McCarthy is a musician, sound designer & composer for stage & screen. He has worked on over ninety theatrical productions, and has collaborated on the making of ten Scotsman Edinburgh Fringe First Award winners. He is also the musical supervisor & co-sound designer on *Pride and Prejudice** (**sort of*), winner of the 2022 Olivier Award for Best Entertainment or Comedy Play.

Other theatre credits include: *The Grand Old Opera House Hotel, Crocodile Fever, Ulster American* (Traverse Theatre); *What Girls Are Made Of* (Traverse Theatre/Raw Materials); *Kidnapped* (National Theatre of Scotland); *Castle Lennox* (Lung Ha Theatre Company/Lyceum Theatre Edinburgh); *Cinderella, Tay Bridge, August: Osage County* (Dundee Rep Theatre) *The Last Return* (Druid Theatre Company); *Nora : A Doll's House* (Young Vic Theatre/Citizens Theatre); *Showtime From The Frontline, The Red Shed* (Mark Thomas); *Jimmy's Hall* (Abbey Theatre).

Work for screen includes the documentaries *Where You're Meant To Be* and *Pitching Up*.

www.michaeljohnmccarthy.com

SIMON JONES – MOVEMENT DIRECTOR

Simon is an award-winning movement director, theatre maker, and lecturer, working across the UK and Europe, focusing heavily on physical storytelling and liveness.

Credits include: *Wendy and Peter Pan* (The Royal Shakespeare Company); *Flathampton* (Royal & Derngate); *Thérèse Raquin* (Theatre Royal Bath); *All That is Solid Melts Into Air, The Hide, One Million,* (Tangled Feet Theatre); *Amphibians, The Drawing Play* (Offstage Theatre); *Moonfleet, The Secret Garden, The Ballad of Martha Brown* (Angel Exit Theatre); *Phone Home, The Situation Room* (Upstart Theatre, Pathos Munich).

Simon collaborates with partner Jennifer Jackson, making new dance-theatre works, including the UK tour of *Endurance*; with the Barbican Theatre's Open Lab on the new work *Wrestle Lads Wrestle*; and his solo piece, *Marco*, supported by ACE and MGCFutures bursary.

Simon is a Lecturer in Movement at The Arden School of Theatre, Manchester, and Associate Artist: Angel Exit, Tangled Feet Theatre, Upstart Theatre, Moving Dust.
www.simoncarrolljones.com

KATE SAGOVSKY – MOVEMENT CONSULTANT

Kate is an artist specialising in somatics, movement, and live performance. She is Artistic Director of performance company MOVING DUST [www.movingdust.com] whose work has been performed to critical acclaim across the UK, including at Soho Theatre, The Bush, Arcola, and Edinburgh Fringe Festival. She has also worked as a movement specialist in many contexts, including at Southbank Centre, Shakespeare's Globe, Royal Shakespeare Company and the National Theatre. Her first book 'Laban's Efforts in Action: A Movement Handbook for Actors' was co-written with Vanessa Ewan and published by Bloomsbury (2019). Kate is Director and Co-Founder of STUDIO SOMA [www.studiosoma.space] an online space for somatic movement.

TINE SELBY – PRODUCTION STAGE MANAGER

Tine is a graduate of the Guildhall School of Music and Drama. Experienced in technical and production management, she has stage managed indoor and outdoor theatre, put power and lights into festivals all around the UK and tour managed national and international theatre shows for Ruby Wax (*Sane New World, Frazzled, How to be Human*) and Mark Thomas (*Bravo Figaro!, Cuckooed, The Red Shed, Showtime from the Frontline, Check Up: Our NHS@70*).

In 2019 she co-founded Tin Cat Entertainment.

HOME

HOME – CO-PRODUCER

HOME is Manchester's centre for international contemporary culture. Since opening in May 2015, HOME has welcomed over four million visitors to its two theatres, five cinemas, art gallery, book shop and restaurants. HOME works with international and UK artists to produce extraordinary theatrical experiences, producing an exciting mix of thought-provoking drama, dance and festivals, with a strong focus on new commissions and talent development. Since opening, HOME has co-produced and co-commissioned work with: Complicité, National Theatre, National Theatre Scotland, Javaad Alipoor, Boy Blue, Hofesh Shechter, Rhum and Clay, Kneehigh, MIF and many more.

HOME's ambition is to push the boundaries of form and technology, to experiment, have fun, take risks and share great new art with the widest possible audience. The patrons of HOME are Danny Boyle, actress Suranne Jones, playwright and poet Jackie Kay CBE, artists Rosa Barba and Phil Collins, filmmaker Asif Kapadia, and actress and author Meera Syal CBE.

homemcr.org
Twitter **@HOME_mcr**
Facebook **/HOMEMcr**
Insta **@homemcr**

TIN CAT ENTERTAINMENT – CO-PRODUCER

Tin Cat is a tour-booking and production company, bringing new, high-quality performances to a variety of venues and audiences. They focus on comedy and theatre that entertains, informs and engages audiences in social and political purpose.

Tin Cat believe the arts can be inspiring and empowering. The performers they work with include Andy Hamilton, Jo Caulfield, Jon Ronson and Mark Thomas.

Tin Cat build strong cultural connections around the UK, to develop long-lasting relationships and give a positive experience to artists, venues, audiences and themselves.

This year they are proud to be co-producing this new play with HOME, Manchester, written by Ed Edwards and directed by Cressida Brown.

tincatentertainment.co.uk
Twitter **@TinCatEnts**
Facebook **/TinCatEntertainment**

**SUPPORTED BY
STONE NEST AND THE STAND COMEDY CLUB**

ENGLAND & SON

Ed Edwards

Special thanks to Eve Steele,
without whose play, *Life By The Throat*,
England & Son could not have been conceived.

Notes

Dialogue or thoughts in italics.

(*Occasional stage directions or clarifications in brackets.*)

Lines can be taken as stage directions as seen fit.

Occasional Headings Or Announcements In Title Case.

This edition features the full-length version of the play.
A slightly abridged version was first performed at the
Edinburgh Festival Fringe.

*This text went to press before the end of rehearsals and so may
differ slightly from the play as performed.*

1.

Beep, beep. Vehicle reversing. Beep Beep...!

Shit!

Dover.

Five a.m.

Paper and carboard piled on top of me. I can't move.

Industrial paper bin. Me inside. Paralysed.

I've got to get out!

Beep, beep!

Bin lorry!

I try to stand.

The *clang-clang* of death approaching.

What's wrong with my legs? *Come on!*

I'm in hell again. Back of Wetherspoons.

I push the lid up. Heave myself over the side. Scrape my shins. Crack my shoulder. Crawl away. Lie there.

Relief.

No one about. Just this yellow jacket looking at me.

Are you alright, mate?

I can't speak.

Yellow jacket calls his mate over.

He must've been sleeping in the bin.

They stare down at me like I'm an insect.

Behind them the giant bin – hotel for the night – ascends above the lorry's crushing jaws.

Industrial *boom*.

The bin shoots its load.

But sudden glimpse.

My best friend Paul – like litter – giant rag doll – still out cold – tumbles into the crusher.

I shout and point. Try to stand.

Arms hold me.

It's all right, mate. Phwoar – he stinks!

My voice grates over the grinding clang.

He's in the lorry! My friend Paul!

They run. Get there too late.

I'm on the ground crying.

Banging my head.

I'm in the shit again.

And I'm not getting out of this one!

Or am I?

Fuck!

Vehicle reversing, reversing, reversing…

2.

My Dad at the Yard.

To distract myself when I'm in the shit, I sometimes try to solve the mystery of my dad when I'm little. When all I want from life is for him to smile at me and ruffle my hair.

Which is hard fucking work.

Example.

(*Gradually becoming his younger self.*)

Me and him – just the two of us – knocking down a building.

My dad does the demolition with a crowbar and a lump hammer while I – aged eight – burn the lead off the brass fittings with a blow torch.

It's great. You hold the brass with tongs and drip the molten lead onto a ladle and make little smooth domes.

I love the blow torch so much I want to burn everything at the yard.

Dad says he knows the feeling but we have to 'show some restraint'.

The lump hammer's good too. It's like a sledgehammer but with a short handle and I can smash whole bricks with it in one go. *Booff!*

Mum says you should always wear goggles when you smash bricks, but Dad says it's fine.

My other jobs – aged eight – are:

Break the mortar off bricks the size of my head. Stack the clean ones and make a mound of rubbish. Sort the zinc and aluminium gullies – butterfly clips – C-clamps – D-clamps…

All day. Nothing goes to waste. Everything will end up in one of Dad's lock-ups.

Three lock-ups he's got. A mile from our house.

One for bricks, slates and masonry. One for ladders and scaffold. One for things Dad calls 'miscellaneous', which I know how to spell and he doesn't.

England used to build things, son, he says. *Now we knock everything down.*

I laugh because England's our name.

England and Son. If we ever go 'legit' Dad says that's what
we'll be called.

In the third lock-up he's got an oil drum. If anything is rusty or
won't come undone – into the oil it goes. Four months later out
it comes. Bingo. Working again.

Anyhow. Back at the yard. Lunch comes. We eat a sandwich.
Nothing.

My dad. Silent as a mountain. Staring at nothing. Definitely not
smiling or ruffling my hair.

Sometimes he nods like he's thinking something. Sometimes he
looks over at me.

Eat up, son.

If his workmates are there they argue about Margaret Thatcher
who's the prime minister.

My dad voted for Margaret Thatcher because he was in the army
once. But he says she betrayed him because she stole his job
when she said she was all about England.

I don't laugh at that England.

Anyhow. By five o'clock the building's gone. I've sorted several
mountains of everything that can be salvaged and put it in the
van. We're covered in muck, I'm proud of myself and I'm
waiting for my reward.

Dad says, *Burn the rubbish*. Gives me some matches. Goes off
to talk money.

The rubbish pile is huge. It's gonna take ages to burn all that.

So I get the petrol can I saw earlier behind the old outhouse and
pour it on the pile.

Over the back. Round the side. The rest on top. And you know,
it's a big can. Almost as big as me.

I don't know my dad's already done this.

And then… (*Strikes a match.*)

How do you describe that sound?

Four streets away they think it's a meteorite.

Next thing I know I'm lying on my back and my dad's staring down at me.

He picks me up. Plonks me on my feet. Probably checking I can stand.

The flames are going up to the sky.

Then it comes.

The smile. Beaming. Laughing smile. Fills up the whole world.

I've got no fucking eyebrows and my dad and everyone from the yard is laughing at me.

But I'm happy because he ruffles what's left of my hair, puts me on his shoulders and we watch it all burn to the ground.

Later my mum shouts about it and my dad goes out on his own.

They're always shouting. Usually it's about money.

Mum says Dad will do anything for money except get a job.

He says where has she been there are no jobs.

She says she's got three.

(*Faint echo of the bin lorry beeping – kept at bay by the next scene.*)

3.

My Dad and the Mystical Power of Learning.

Dad always says, *Education's the only way out, son*.

I always think, *Out of what?*

He takes lessons himself. *Make sure you're doing it right*.

His favourite is the Greek Myths because: *It's what educated people learn.*

But worst of all. He comes in to speak to my teacher.

This great big bloke. Donkey jacket the size of Balham. Putrefying the air with some stink from the yards. Striding up the playground to Miss Jones. Object of my prepubescent stirrings of wonder.

'Scuse me love. Can you help me with some pedagogy?

Miss Jones pulls a strange face. All the kids laugh.

Is that funny man your dad?

No.

But if I try hard Dad ruffles my hair. So when I'm eight I'm a good boy. Top of the class.

All the dreams he has left in life are for me.

It was just never gonna happen.

4.

Beep-beep!! – Beep-beep…!!

5.

My Dad in the West End.

He does the doors at the theatre sometimes. After he's finished at the yard. Sometimes he wears a top hat. Tonight it's just the livery and a bit of braid.

He says, *I was a soldier once. Then I made cars. Now look at me.* (*Meaning: dressed like a clown.*)

I think, *He does look smart in that clobber.*

I don't remember why I'm there that night but I do remember I'm eating a raspberry ripple tub with a little wooden spoon one of the girls with the trays always gives me.

My two favourite things. Raspberry ripple and my dad.

Except for the blow torch.

And the lump hammer.

Anyway. A car pulls up and my dad looks down at me.

There's four men in the car. One of them winds the window down and says something to my dad about some money.

My dad ignores the man. Talks to me.

Go inside. Find the woman who gave you the ice cream. Stay inside.

I go through the big doors, but stop and look back. He's watching me.

He signals, *Go!*

I sneak round to the side door and peer through the glass.

A Scene.

The man from the car window out now. Waving his arms around.

My dad. Looking down at the man like he wants to put a collar on him and take him for a walk.

My dad says something. The man with the arms nods.

My dad comes into the foyer. Goes into the loo on the ground floor. Comes out a minute later with a massive iron bayonet from a First World War rifle.

It looks heavy.

Later I think, *How was there a massive iron bayonet from a First World War rifle in the toilet of a West End theatre?* He must have had it hidden in there.

My dad's face is calm. But he looks like someone else.

I watch through the side door. Cold glass on my forehead.

He strides past the man with the arms to the front of the car.

And then. Moment stuck in time forever. His hand goes up in the air – fist on metal – ancient amulet – and – *crash*!

Bayonet on glass.

Windscreen holds. But cracks mightily.

Statues of people in the street. Staring.

Then *crash* – and *crash*!

Windscreen surrenders to the force.

I'm like that. (*Gawping*.)

The men from the back seat get out now and wave their arms too and shout.

There's a crowd of people watching. Some of them fall away in a wave with the crashes.

I hear what the man with the arms is shouting now.

Do you know who we are?

My dad walks to the front of the car – like he's just working at the yard – smashes the headlights.

Bash. Bosh.

Indicators.

Tinkle. Clink.

It was a gorgeous little car before that. Shining in the coloured lights.

The guy in the driver's seat gets out now too but my dad traps him in the car door.

Then some people block my view and I have to dash outside.

When I get there the man from the driver's seat is dangling from my dad's fist by his collar and my dad's slamming the car door on his head.

Bam – bam – bam.

The other men aren't waving their arms now. They're saying things quietly to my dad.

My dad lets the man from the car door go and they all move away backwards together like a man with four heads.

One of them has my dad's big bayonet but he's just holding it, and he shouts again:

Do you know who we are!

My dad just stands there waving, with this crooked smile I've never seen before.

Bye bye.

Then he turns and holds out his hand for me to take.

We don't normally hold hands when we walk along the road, but we do that night.

I look up at him.

Mythical beast. Minotaur. Leviathan.

Do your homework.

6.

My Dad and the Shooting.

We're on holiday in a caravan in Tenby. Or it might be Cromer. Mum's cooking sausage and chips.

Mum's always happy in my holiday memories – and my dad isn't quiet.

Dad says, *Name three essential raw materials that go into making cars*.

I'm eight so I'm still trying to impress him.

Rubber. Chromium. Bauxite. (Pron: Borks-ite.)

Good boy, he says.

Why is hair ruffling so powerful?

And where does it all come from?

It comes from South Africa, Guinea and Malaysia – and you've been to all of them!

Dad always tells army stories at tea time on holiday. Malaya's my favourite.

Independent Malaya united with the then British crown colonies of North Borneo, Sarawak, and Singapore on the 16th of September 1963 to become Malaysia. I actually shout that.

My dad's beaming.

He loves it, doesn't he. My little soldier.

Malaya goes like this. I join in with the lines…

Dad says, *Sergeant Jones was a bar-stud!*

We look at Mum.

Mum pretends to disapprove of swearing. But Dad's allowed to swear when he tells army stories on holiday.

Proper bar-stud Sergeant Jones. 'Get in that lorry Bulldog –'

Bulldog's what they called my dad in the army. Basher's his best mate. Bulldog and Basher.

'Get in that lorry now, Bulldog, or I'll run you through the chicken wire so hard you'll come out the other side chips!'

I shout the 'chips' with him.

And why don't you argue with Sergeant Jones?

I look at Mum. She nods.

Because he's a bar-stud!

Correct. Now, normally when we set off in the lorry we're laughing and joking. But not today, son. Why not?

Because of the look on Sergeant Jones's face.

Correct. And what do the lads always say?

'When Sergeant Jones <u>looks</u> grim – it's gonna <u>get</u> grim.'

But we're in for a surprise that day, aren't we, son.

Yes. Because it was just a 'peaceful demonstration'.

Exactly. It's just this bunch of skinny little men, nearly in the nude, shouting and waving banners. But then who turns up to put the cat among the pigeons?

I like this bit. I shout: *Adolf Hitler!*

You naughty boy. This isn't Nazi Germany! This is Malaya and we're honourable Englishmen. I think you mean Captain Nigel Stilton-Cheese!

I laugh. *That's not his real name.*

Oh sorry, son. I mean Captain Nigel Stanton-Cleaves. Grandson of the fifth Earl of Nowhere! And what are his orders?

He says to open fire.

*

(Malaya.)

Live rounds!

Load!

Fire!

*

(Back to Cromer – or Tenby.)

But do the regiment obey these orders, son?

Yes, Dad. Some of them do.

But what do <u>most</u> of us do? Because we're Englishmen and Englishmen are gentlemen.

You fire in the air over their heads to scare them away.

Dad readies himself for the end of the story. Adjusting his enormous form in the miniscule caravan seat. Tattoo on one arm, scar on the other.

And what is the moral of this fine story? he says.

I say, 'When Sergeant Jones looks grim…'

No, son.

That is definitely the right answer. I look at him, puzzled.

Think about it. Why am I there in the first place?

He's got a new look on his face. Not the normal one from holiday.

Teacher.

Oracle.

And I get it. *Rubber, chromium, bauxite!*

Cammere…! (Big hair ruffle.)

Always remember, son, when you buy a car, England chipped in.

I laugh.

And a few years later – when we steal our first car – I remember this aphorism fondly.

As we screech away I say – (*Impression of his dad.*) *Always remember, Paul, when you steal a car, England stole it in the first place.*

Paul laughs and says, *What the fuck are you on?*

7.

Beep beep…

Sound of a police interview recorder being turned on…

VOICE (*faintly heard*). *Interview commencing at 13.15…*

8.

Dad's Friend from the Army.

I'm in Wetherspoons with Basher when I find out what really happened in Malaya.

Years fucking later. The key to the mystery.

Curry night.

Basher has the chicken madras. I have sausage and chips.

I've just got out of jail again.

How did you find the food in there? Basher says.

I shrug, *Same as usual.*

I'm here on condition he doesn't talk about my dad.

But as soon as there's an awkward pause it starts.

Malaya was hell, Basher says. *We were young. They'd call it PTSD now. I'm not making excuses.*

You saw bad things, I say – desperate to stop him.

Yes, he says. *But that's not really it.*

He puts his fork down carefully. I brace myself.

It's more. How do I put it? You do bad things.

It's the first time in years I've thought about my dad. *Why the fuck did I come?*

It's what you're there for, Basher says. *What you're there to <u>do</u>.*

To lighten it, I say, *Stilton-Cheese*.

Basher's face changes. Like a smile breaking through granite.

He was a bar-stud.

I laugh. *I thought that was Sergeant Jones?*

No. No, Jones was a <u>kant</u>. Stilton-Cheese was the bar-stud. Fucking Earl of summing-summing – related to Churchill. Listen, why don't you have a drink?

I haven't had one since I got out because I know where it ends up.

He says, *Best thing about Wetherspoons, the cheap-but-quality beer.*

I say, *Yes*. Meaning the cheap-but-quality beer.

Camming up! he says and skips to the bar.

Pint and a shot. Each.

I leave mine on the table. He won't even notice.

Me and your old man – do you mind me talking about him?

I shake my head stupidly.

What a bloke. What a bloke. Not like the rest of us, Bulldog.

He goes on and on about him. I take a sip.

Everyone looked up to him. Sergeant Jones was terrified of him.

Fuck it. Down in one.

Atta boy! Basher says.

And the shot.

Four rounds later. Or is it five? It pours out of him.

Malaya. Kenya. Oman. All over the Empire me and Bulldog are. I know we don't call it that any more, but who owns the banks and the businesses – eh? Haha. Legalised robbery really, init eh? Cheers.

But your old man. He was something else. They encouraged him. Made his own weapons he did. Personal meat cleaver. Hand-crafted shillelagh. Bulldog: God of war! People don't understand. It's what you're there for…

I don't know how it happens but a few pints after that I'm holding a photograph. Scruffy black-and-white photo. Cracked like a pirate's face.

Jungle scene. A young man in khaki uniform. Posing proudly for the camera.

And I know that crooked smile.

Malaya, Basher says. *It was hell.*

The man with the crooked smile is holding two severed heads by the hair.

9.

Paul.

I'm fourteen when I'm taken from my children's home near Dartmoor to the juvenile detention centre.

Brainchild of Margaret Thatcher's Home Secretary – The Viscount Willie Whitelaw – I give you –

The Short Sharp Shock.

Children's homes feel pretty much the same as jail, so to make jail feel worse for the likes us, we were going to face The Wrath of the Mighty.

Run by ex-military personnel, the short sharp shock is designed to instil discipline and keep wayward youths on the path of righteousness.

What could go wrong?

I don't remember what I've done this time but let's just say mine and Paul's stealing is definitely <u>not</u> legalised.

In reception one of the officers very politely asks me my name.

When I tell him he punches me in the face.

Bam!

He's a big guy. As big as my dad.

I burst into tears.

And I swear by Almighty God I will never cry again!

As I come out with my scratchy blankets I see Paul who got here yesterday.

He's standing in the corridor completely naked where he's been stood for twenty-four hours and where everyone who works there has to walk past him.

10.

There's so many kids in the place they have to put us on the men's wing.

Just me and Paul two-ed up together.

We were best friends before. We're brothers now.

First night. Middle of winter. No drugs.

Paul says, *Can I get in with you? I'm freezing.*

I say, *In my bed?*

He says, *Yeah.*

I say, *Okay.*

He falls asleep straight away while I remember:

The First Time I Stand Up To My Dad.

He's shouting at my mum in the kitchen and she's crying but he won't stop.

It's about my stealing again. How it's all her fault because she spoils me.

I feel like my teeth are going to break.

Normally I run out of the house till it gets dark. Or if I'm in bed I block my ears.

Sometimes I piss myself and hide my sheets in the cupboard.

Tonight I step in between them, push him and roar:

You're a bar-stud!

He stops and looks down at me.

He gets the reference. I see it hit home.

My mum's hands are on my shoulders and she says, *It's okay, go out and play now.*

My dad's face looks like rocks.

I shout, *Leave her alone!* – and push him again.

Mum's watching him too. I can tell.

Big man, he says.

I see his broken tooth.

It's a smile. The crooked one.

Put your shoes on.

I don't want to move because of Mum but he steps back to show me it's okay.

Mum mouths something to me secretly.

Run.

I shake my head.

He's a big man now, my dad says.

It's cold and I'm shaking.

He gets his van keys from the hook.

Mum says, *Please don't.*

He says, *Shh…!*

*

My dad's quiet in the van.

The lights from the lamp posts look like insects rushing over us and I know where we're going now.

When we get there the yard looks different. I've never been here at night.

There's a train passing in the distance.

He opens one of the lock-ups and I get it now.

He gestures and I go in.

He closes the door behind me and locks it from the outside.

I wait until I hear the van drive off then I piss in the oil drum where the rusty bolts go. Later I shit in the corner and I sleep under the ripped tarpaulins and something really bad's gonna happen and Paul's shaking me saying,

Mate, you're shouting. It's okay. It's okay.

It's okay.

My breathing slows down and Paul makes me laugh about stealing and sex and after a bit he says, *If you close your eyes, my hand would feel like a girl's.*

I say, *I'm not fucking gay!*

He says, *Neither am I!*

I say, *If you tell anyone I'll kill you.*

He says, *If you tell anyone I'll kill you.*

11.

The next day on the landing the worst screw in the nick makes a beeline for me. With two of his mates.

He's known for shoving soap up your arse this screw. And making you stand to attention till you shit yourself.

Paul throws a chair at him before he gets to me and they beat Paul so badly he limps for the rest of his life.

I get the soap treatment the next day instead.

And I swear by almighty God. When the fat screw gets me round the neck. And the nasty one plonks the metal bucket in front of me. And shows me the soap. And disappears behind me. And shoves it up me as hard as he can. And stands me to attention while the fat screw pulls my pants up. And his head's next to my dick...

I do not make one single fucking sound.

12.

The Miracle.

After my Short Sharp Shock there's not one thing in the whole wide world that can touch me.

Except a miracle.

I'm sent back to the kids' home near Dartmoor that looks like a ruined castle –

Did I mention they move us all to Devon?

In the late 1980s – after a few years of Thatcher stealing everyone's jobs – the kids' homes in the cities are full. So we – the bad kids of London, Liverpool and Manchester – are transported in our thousands to the south of lovely old England.

I reckon some well-meaning social worker says, *I know, nice clean air'll do them good. We love hiking, don't we, Helen.*

So we all end up in the nice clean air.

And rob the bastards blind.

13.

Which is where I've been when The Miracle comes.

Hotel on the front.

Paul's the full 'Mr Shady' so he only has to stand in reception and I'm invisible.

In he goes. Looks around. All the eyes go *beeeep* – (*On Paul.*)

I'm up the stairs – out the window – onto the fire escape – along the roof – pop the skylight – down.

Four hundred quid in cash sitting there on the side. Knife through creamy butter.

I'm back in time for tea and there's this woman there.

Beautiful woman. Staring at me.

I mean she's nearly thirty or something – like a proper woman – but I'm stunned.

Her clothes are hippy-but-not-quite. Hard to describe. Couple of dreadlocks at the side.

I'm trying not to stare when she says my name and I think, *Shit, she's undercover, I'm nicked!*

But she's grinning this massive grin.

It's you isn't it, she says.

I shrug. Or well my shoulders twitch anyway.

She comes over and stands right in front of me.

It's embarrassing and nice at the same time.

Then she touches my cheek with the back of her hand and bursts into tears!

I want to cry too, but *I swore by almighty God.*

She asks Mike the care worker if it's really me and he says, *It's him alright.*

It's Martha, she says. *I was your social worker when you were five. I used to take you to school. I held your hand while you walked on the walls and we sang 'Ghost Town'. Don't you remember?*

Then she sings the first line.

(*Sings it.*)

The skin on my neck prickles because I do remember singing that with someone on the way to school.

But a social worker?

When I was five?

(*She sings the haunting line about 'the good old days'.*)

How are you? she says.

Good, I say.

And I really fucking mean it.

You were so cute, she says. *Such a beautiful boy.*

The way she says it I believe her.

She says, *I've found you now and you are not getting away this time!*

14.

My Mum.

Normally when I'm spooked I climb out the window and go and meet everyone.

But tonight I smoke a spliff and stare at the mad twisted stone on the ceiling in my room.

I'm thinking about Martha – course I am. But there's something else.

After she sees me, Martha stays for tea and after tea she says, *Do you want to come for a drive?*

Deux-chevaux, her car's called. Two horse-power in French.

It's got mad folding windows and string door handles and the engine sounds weird. But it's sunny and we're smoking Camel cigarettes and I'm talking about myself.

I don't do that.

I mean. They make me talk to people all the time but I don't say anything.

I tell her which kids' homes I've been in and who was nice and she gets angry when I tell her who wasn't. Or about being locked in my room at night in the secure units.

Fucking bastards, she says, *You can't be convicted of a crime in some countries till you're sixteen!*

I say, *Which ones, I'm going there*, and she laughs.

She says she's been travelling. India, Vietnam, Malaysia.

I say, *Independent Malaya united with the then British Crown colonies of North Borneo, Sarawak, and Singapore on the sixteenth of September 1963 to become Malaysia.*

She laughs. *You were always clever. Did you learn that at school?*

I say, *My dad was in Malaya.*

She nods. Says nothing.

When it was becoming Malaysia.

My breathing's gone weird.

I don't know what this is suddenly. This sun and the blue sky and the lane going past and flicking my ash out the window.

She lets me be quiet.

I see her knee glowing orange in the sunlight.

I don't want to think that she doesn't shave her legs and there's darker hair on her shins but the little hairs on the inside of her knee are lighter.

But I do.

I'm thinking about it again now. On my bed in the dark. With the light from the porch shining on the ceiling.

Spooked.

I jump up and turn the light on.

Why don't I go out and get pissed? I've got the money.

Fuck it. Spliff. Lights out. Get into bed.

I need to remember.

15.

I'm back under the ripped tarpaulins in the lock-up. Aged eleven.

Something bad's gonna happen.

It's my mum.

*

She's wearing sunglasses in the house.

*

I hear her screaming downstairs from my bed.

*

I'm sitting on her knee after school and she's kissing me, saying, *He's a bastard, I hate him.* Her breath smells.

*

She takes the sheets out of my wardrobe and gives me a look.

*

She's lying on the floor.

My dad says, *Leave her there, she's pissed.*

*

She's hugging and kissing me and saying, *I love you.*

My arms are by my sides and I'm not moving.

*

My dad is shouting outside in the street. *You dirty fucking bitch!*

She shouts, *You don't own me!*

He shouts, *Oh yes I do!*

*

I remember Dad taking me to the cliffs at Dover.

Up to the edge.

He puts his hand on the back of my neck and I can lean right over.

I get scared and say, *Can we go home now?*

He says, *Shhh.*

And I do go *Shhh.*

*

We're in the park. I'm cold and I'm crying.

Mum says, *Please be quiet!*

Later she's in the lake and I'm shouting to her but she can't hear me.

Two policemen are in the water with her.

When she comes out we have silver blankets and they let me use the radio in the police car.

*

Mum pushes Dad in our kitchen.

He gets his arm round her neck and she stamps and shouts and kicks him.

When he lets go she throws boiling water at him from the kettle.

He screams and grabs her round the neck again.

*

The police are talking to my mum in the kitchen.

The policewoman closes the door.

*

I'm skipping and my mum's turning the rope. The other end's on the door knob.

I had a little bubble car, number forty-eight, I took it round the coorrrner. And slammed on the brakes.

*

I'm coming down the curly slide at the open-air baths.

Mum is clapping me.

*

We look at her and she nods.

I say, *Sergeant Jones was a bar-stud!*

*

We're on the beach.

Dad has his hand on her leg under the towel. She squeals and laughs.

*

We're in the car.

The windscreen wipers are on. My dad has his hand on her leg again.

*

Dad's banging on the bathroom door saying, *I love you*.

I come out onto the landing.

Dad is crying and saying he's sorry. I've never seen him cry before.

I don't like it.

*

Mum's going down the path with a big bag and he's pulling her back to the house shouting, *Get back in there!*

She looks up at the window and sees me watching.

*

There's a noise outside.

I'm back in the lock-up under the ripped tarpaulins aged eleven.

I've been shut in here for two days and two nights and the door is rattling in the dark.

Mum's outside. Shaking the door. Calling my name.

I hear his van on the gravel. He beeps his horn.

She's shouting at him over the engine as it revs.

It's dark but I can see light from the headlights.

The engine stops.

Shadows flicker in the door cracks.

I'm scared.

Mum is talking to me through the door. She says, *I'm sorry, son.*

I say, *You haven't done anything*.

She says, '*Not doing anything*' *is the problem*.

I realise this is the last thing she ever says to me and I sit up and shout, *Paul!*

16.

I'm downstairs in the laundry later that night.

Mike the social worker says, *You're doing a wash at this time?*

I nod.

He says, *You're growing up*.

I don't tell him it's my sheets.

17.

Martha's Place.

You can smoke spliff when you're with me, Martha says the first time I stay over at her house. *I'm not your social worker.*

It sounds funny when she says it. 'Smoke spliff.' I laugh and feel like a kid.

Then I roll a spliff.

I offer her some but she shakes her head. I know she smokes it. I've seen her tin.

I feel weird doing it on my own so I only have a bit.

But it's her house that really throws me.

It's this tiny little place down a path at the edge of a village and I can't suss it out.

I mean, she's got money. Her mum's rich. But her mum's place is like all the other big houses down here – and I know what everything is in them houses.

To the penny. Every stick.

It's all in *Miller's Antique Handbook and Price Guide*.

Beautifully photographed with fact-reference boxes.

Over eight thousand collectable items. Soft-paste porcelain. Oriental furniture. Peers and consoles. Clothes-presses. Overmantle mirrors. Byzantine clocks.

Indian jewellery. Civil war fire-guards. Antique teddy bears. Taiwanese tea sets. All the gold and south American silver ever stolen from a Chinese trading ship by a European pirate in every shape and setting. Plus prices.

Paul's a genius at locks and climbing but once we're in he's like, *Grab something, come on!*

For me it's *Miller's Guide*.

I take my time. Get the feel of the place. Look stuff up.

These houses are literally made of money.

Sublimely tasteful bling.

Eighteen months of *Miller's Antique Handbook and Price Guide* reveals this world to me in all its greedy grace.

I do my homework.

A jeweller in Tintagel melts down the gold and silver while I wait.

Ceramics to a lock-up behind a garage in Winchester.

Oriental furniture to Singapore via a shop in Worthing.

All over the south of England I am.

Sales of *Miller's Guide* go through the roof so the dealers can keep up with me. This kid from south London.

Anyhow. Martha's house has none of that.

There's not one single thing I recognise from any house I've ever been in before.

It's beautiful and different and I feel strangely at home.

18.

The second time I stay for the weekend – or it might be the third – Martha takes me to the Old Quarry.

I can't believe it when we get there.

There's cliffs all the way round this crystal, bottomless pool. Ancient trees at the top. Sun glinting on the water. No one for miles.

Martha says, *Well?*

I say, *Fuck-in-nell!*

We've squeezed through a gap in the rocks and we're on this stone platform halfway down one side.

I notice the quiet.

Martha plonks the bags down. Takes all her clothes off. Charges naked to the edge and dives into the void.

It's fucking ages before there's a splash and a – *Whoop!* – when she comes up.

Which I don't see cos I'm still standing there like that. (*Gobsmacked.*)

I come to the edge and she shouts, *Come on!*

I see her in the water. All green and white. Like a mermaid.

Dark patch between her legs.

It's a <u>long</u> way down.

I say, *How the fuck do you get out?*

She points at a rusty old ladder further along.

I take a few minutes to pluck up the courage. But then I dive –
in swim shorts she's lent me – and *crash*.

When we get out I go first so I don't have to walk behind
her – and we fling ourselves off the edge again and again. All
afternoon. Till we're knackered.

Then we lie in the sun.

She's still naked but I don't look.

I mean. I don't stare.

I mean. She never wears a bra anyway so it's not like I haven't
caught a glimpse before.

And I'm not stupid. I know she's trying to show me things can
be different. Like a lesson. And I do want that. I do.

But later. In bed. I imagine if I'd gone in naked myself. And I
think what if it wasn't a lesson?

I picture us swimming over to the rocks on the other side.
Getting out. Sitting together.

But then I feel weird so I get up and smoke a spliff instead.

Then I start thinking about my mum again so I find the vodka
she keeps in the freezer and drink it.

19.

Next morning Martha cooks a massive breakfast with
Sainsbury's Taste the Difference Tropical Juice and she says,
How would you feel about me fostering you?

I say, *You mean, come here and live with you?*

She says, *Yes.*

I say, *Just me and you?*

She says, *Yes.*

I must have gone quiet because she says, *It's okay you can think about it.*

I say, *I don't need to, I'd like that.*

20.

Paul's staying with us for the weekend.

Martha's scared of Paul because she knows what we get up to together. But she says she wants to get to know him because she knows I love him.

I laugh and picture his mad dancing when we go out. Jail. His Mr Shady act.

Like family, she says.

I say, *Yes, I love him.*

After tea on the first night Paul rolls a spliff, offers it to Martha and she takes it.

She doesn't look right doing it. And I don't like the way she laughs and touches Paul's arm. But I can tell he likes her so I'm glad.

That night on the floor in my room Paul says, *You'd better not fuck this up with her.*

I say, *I won't.*

He says, *You might.*

I say, *I know.*

He says, *I'm not coming again, I'm a bad influence.*

And he doesn't.

21.

I'm coming out of the sea with her.

She's teaching me to surf and I'm pretty good already.

Her three best mates are there.

She calls them *The Lost Girls* because they've got everything but feel like they've got nothing.

They dress like she does and they're beautiful too.

They clap and cheer as we approach.

I do a funny dance and they laugh.

The one I really like says, *The best surfer on the beach is the one who's having the most fun.*

I think, *That's definitely me.*

I lie in the sun with my head next to Martha's legs and listen to them talk about going to Kenya and Jamaica and Cyprus and South Africa.

22.

Martha's friend Bob gives me a job at his boat yard.

They call themselves 'artisans'.

Martha says that means posh people doing working-class things, charging more and doing a worse job.

I make the tea and take deliveries and push the boats around. Which is a bit boring. But Bob's nice and he shows me how to polish the hulls on the racing catamarans which look amazing.

He says, *If you know boats you can work all over the world.* Even Singapore. Like he did for five years.

I show Bob all the ways you can break into his yard and steal everything.

He looks shocked but I help him make it safer. Then he takes me to his friend's yard which is even worse.

His friend says, *Who'd want to steal this stuff anyway*.

I say, *You'd be surprised*.

He gives me a look.

But actually I haven't stolen anything for nine months, three weeks and two days. Which should be in the Guinness Book of Fucking Records.

23.

Martha's teaching me to make vegetarian lasagne.

I say, *Did you ever meet my mum before she was killed?*

She says, *Your mum was lovely. She was very pretty and she laughed a lot.*

I say, *I remember her shouting a lot.*

She says, *What else do you remember about her?*

I say, *I remember her tying the skipping rope to the door knob.*

Martha says, *I think that might have been me.*

Then she sings, *I had a little bubble car number forty-eight, I took it round the corrrrner.*

I burst into tears.

She puts her arms round me and I smell her beautiful smell.

24.

We've come home drunk after a barbecue on the beach.

I've just cleaned my teeth and I'm in my boxers.

Martha's in bed laughing at my impressions of The Lost Girls.

I end up getting in with her. Which I do sometimes. But when she turns the light off somehow her boob ends up pressing against the back of my hand.

I can feel it moving when she laughs.

I keep my hand there for ages. But then I realise it's not her boob. It's just the soft bit of her arm.

I laugh and she says, *What?*

I say, *Nothing.*

She says, *Tell me.*

I say, *I can't.*

She says, *You've got to tell me now!*

So I do.

She goes quiet and I can hear her breathing.

She says, *You know we can't do anything like that, don't you.*

I say, *Course!*

She says, *You know why?*

I say, *Yeah.*

But later I think, *Actually I don't know why.* And I wonder if it's illegal.

It probably is.

But so's stealing.

25.

I've bought Martha her favourite bottle of very-expensive-wine with my own-actual-money that I earned at the boat yard.

Bob had to go in and get it for me because I still don't look old enough.

But when I get home there's this cute woman's car on the drive. And when I go inside Martha looks different.

I say, *What's up?*

She says, *Nothing.*

I laugh and say, *You've got to tell me now!*

Then I realise there's a guy there.

Martha says, *This is my boyfriend, Anthony.*

Anthony with a 'th' in the middle. Who builds luxury boats and who's been in Saudi Arabia for eighteen months.

She's told me about him a couple of times but.

He's looking at me. And I know that look from jail. Not that he's ever done any time.

It says, *Who The Fuck Are You?*

I say, *Is that your car outside?*

He says, *No, that's a present for Martha.*

After tea Martha rolls a spliff from her tin and laughs and touches Anthony's arm a lot.

In the morning she says, *We're going swimming at the Old Quarry, do you want to come?*

I say, *Nah I might meet Paul.*

She says, *That's nice. Give him my love.*

26.

Me and Paul are being chased through Tintagel by five cops and we've had it this time.

But then Paul shouts, *Go fucking home!* – and stops.

He puts the first copper through a sweet-shop window so the rest have to stop and tackle him.

Five of them it takes. Well four. The first one's still bleeding into a tray of fudge.

By which time I'm long gone.

Paul tells me the details when I visit him in jail. He gets a long one for that.

He says, *You're fucking it up, aren't you.*

I say, *Yeah.*

Martha puts money in his private cash and sends him a thank you card.

27.

Martha's gone away with Anthony for a week so I'm staying at Martha's mum's house.

I like Sylvia a lot and she likes me.

She's impressed by my in-depth knowledge of Oriental furniture. Of which her house is chocka-fucking-block.

She shows me the family jewellery and I can ID every piece and give her a price.

Sylvia checks in her *Miller's Guide* and I'm right every time. Which makes her laugh.

Her laugh's exactly like Martha's and I can't help it but when she opens the safe I note the combination.

Later when we're 'having tea' I spot an old photo on the Arts and Crafts William Morris Repo sideboard and go over.

Black-and-white jungle scene. Dark-skinned men with no shirts. Big English gentleman posing grandly in the middle.

I say, *Malaya?*

Martha's granddad, she says. *How did you know?*

Dunno.

She says, *He stayed through the Emergency. I was born over there and so was Martha. Father used to say 'They'll kill us all and steal everything'.* Meaning the communists. Of course they never did.

I say, *Bauxite?*

She says, *No rubber. We make hoovers there now too, can you believe. Not me, obviously. The family business.*

28.

The End Comes.

It's the fourth time I've 'disappeared' in six weeks and I'm in this big house in Exmoor when I see it.

Queen-Anne-style, *Escritoire.*

I get a thump in my chest and scrabble for the secret compartment. They all have one.

I find the key to the safe. And in the safe there's this egg.

I drive to London. Cash it in for twenty grand. Burn through the lot in ten days.

Dancing. Drinking. Falling over.

I try heroin for the first time.

I drive to back Paul's friend's squat in Devon and stay for a week raving and having sex with a girl I don't really like.

When I get back Martha cries again and says, *Where have you been?*

I say, *All over.*

She says, *You should have let me know were okay.*

I say, *Why? You're not my mum.*

She gets this look on her face I've never seen before.

Later in bed I hear them arguing about me.

Anthony says, *He doesn't give a shit about you.*

Martha says, *He needs me.*

Anthony says, *He's a grown man.*

She says, *You don't understand him.*

He says, *He's a dangerous dog and you're only not scared cos he eats your biscuits.*

Martha cries.

I sneak to the freezer but no vodka.

I do a line of whizz instead. Which is stupid because then I have to listen to them fucking all night.

29.

The next day I 'go missing' again. But Martha comes to Paul's friend's squat and brings me home.

Her face is so sad in the car I want to touch it.

I also want to punch it.

30.

I try to dream about travelling to Singapore and Jamaica but I never get further than some big house with tasteful bling.

Then there's arguing again and make-up sex and one day I sit Martha down at her kitchen table of unknown provenance and say,

I'm leaving.

She says, *No you're not.*

I say, *I can't do this.*

She says, *Yes you can.*

I say, *I'm messing things up.*

She says, *I don't care.*

I say, *I can't do that to you.*

She says, *You're not doing it. They are.*

I say, *Who is?*

She says, *The bastards who run everything.*

I say, *The ones whose houses I rob?*

She says, *Yes!*

I say, *People like Sylvia?*

She gets a funny look on her face but says, *Probably, yes.*

We have this argument ten different ways on ten different days.

She sends Anthony away.

She says she'll leave him because I'm more important.

But on the tenth day I pack my stuff and go.

On the doorstep she grips me so hard I nearly cry.

She says, *I love you. Come back whenever you want.*

The next weekend I break into her mum's house and empty the safe.

31.

I'm outside Tesco's where Martha shops on Saturdays crying behind the barbecues and logs.

*

I cry as she gets into her cute little car at the boat yard where she does the books on Tuesdays.

*

I'm outside Drucker's. Tears streaming down my face. She meets her mum there Fridays.

Her mum cries that day too.

*

I make sure she never sees me but I follow Martha everywhere she goes for a month.

Crying.

*

I go big.

Ees. Whizz. Acid.

Then smack. Then crack. Then both.

*

There's an underground labyrinth connecting the crack houses of England that only the undead can see.

At first you go in sometimes.

Then you live there.

*

When I'm on smack I sleep with my trainers under my head and my drugs down my pants.

*

When I'm on crack I steal trainers from under people's heads and drugs from down their pants.

*

I know I love crack because one night – when I need a fantasy – instead of Martha or The Lost Girls – I picture a rock of it glowing red on a bed of ash and it makes me come.

*

Sometimes in the labyrinth I bump into Paul and we hang out.

Then we fight and go our separate ways.

We always fight when we're drunk.

*

The only way out is jail.

Get down the gym.

Get big.

Read.

Get out.

*

In Bournemouth I watch two men fight to the death over a fifteen-pound bag.

When they're done the victor smears the blood of the vanquished on a sleeping junkie and we all get off.

*

In Brighton I have sex with a woman who steals my drugs and goes over.

I don't realise she's dead till morning when I need to score so l leave her there.

*

In Bristol we rush a place where gay men meet and rob two guys.

They look scared.

I say sorry but keep the money.

*

Years pass in seconds.

Decades pass in minutes.

I'm shrink-wrapped by time.

*

In Liverpool a group of men rush in with baseball bats and smash my knee, my shin and my elbow.

*

In Manchester someone sets fire to my tent.

I lose my ear, my hair on this side, and my eye won't close properly.

*

But Dover. (*Relief.*)

Down the alley at the back of Wetherspoons there's three lock-ups exactly like my dad's.

In the first are the smack heads. The second, alkies. The third, migrants.

We are The Demolished.

And even though we rob them and fight – and bring it on top with the law – the migrants look out for us.

They don't understand us. Even though one or two of them have a sneaky bag now and then. But they pick us up off the ground and tend our wounds.

Once they take me round the back and break my nose because I've overstepped the mark.

Afterwards we're mates. But less.

It's why I always end up in Dover.

Thirty-Two

Beep beep… Beep beep… Beep beep…

(*We're back at the start. Re-enacting Scene 1. Getting out of the bin, crawling away…*)

Shit!

I've got to get out!

Are you alright, mate?

Phwoar – he stinks!

It's all right, mate.

He's in there!

What's he say?

Dunno.

In the bin lorry! My friend Paul!

(*This suddenly looks like CCTV rewound and stopped – and we're in court.*)

The smug bastard in the wig is talking to me.

That's you, isn't it, sir? The man who climbed out of the bin and crawled away?

I say, *It looks like me but it isn't me.*

(*To audience.*) Which is the statutory defense.

I feel a dick saying it. But you saw it. Paul fell in the lorry. That's how he died.

Wiggy Bastard looks smug.

The judge looks down and writes something.

Wiggy says, *Can we play the first clip again, please? From two hours previously. Two thirty-five a.m.?*

Click.

The man-who-looks-like-me is very, very drunk. He has something heavy in his hand and is banging a-man-who-looks-like-Paul on the head with it until the-man-who-looks-like-Paul is on the ground, not moving.

It looks like me but it isn't me.

Click. Ten minutes later.

The man-who-looks-like-me takes ages to heave the man-who-looks-like-Paul into an industrial paper bin.

(*To the audience.*) You all look at me like I'm a monster.

I understand what you think you're seeing, but…

Click.

The man-who-looks-like-me is on the ground asleep for ages. Then he wakes up and climbs into the paper bin himself.

Then we're back where we started.

Wiggy says, *You killed him, didn't you, sir.*

I stare at him.

And you all stare at me. Like a person with twelve heads.

The judge tells me to answer the question.

On remand you go over and over stuff but when you get to court they get in your head and I can't help it, I shout,

You wiggy fucking bastard it's **not** *fucking me!*

Wiggy sits down. *No further questions, your honour.*

33.

I get fourteen years for killing Paul.

I fight a lot at first so I'm ghosted to jails all over the country.

I wreck my knuckles and break my jaw. Someone slices my cheek open. I get another eight years in outside court for gouging the guy's eye out.

Until I end up in this old fort on the edge of an ancient marsh in the middle of nowhere with a special wing for ex-army prisoners.

A whole wing of killers who can't stop killing just because they've stopped being paid to do it.

And I know my dad's here. I can feel it.

First day. I'm on the block already. Hatch slides open.

I knew it was you! I told 'em it was. No one believed me, but I knew!

It's the first familiar voice I've heard in months.

I hear you was arrested behind Wetherspoons! Not the one we went to, I hope? Hahaha. Love that place.

It's the cheap-but-quality beer, I say.

And curry night. Don't forget curry night. There's one down the road. We go every Thursday. How are you anyway?

Good, I say.

Good lad, good lad. Nice little job for ex-army like me, this. A few of us in this place, if you get my drift. Both sides of the door.

I nod.

Basher says, *They're good lads mostly. On the other side.*

Except they've done bad things, I say.

Basher nods.

Very bad thigs, I say. *Unforgiveable things. It's why they're in here.*

Yes, Basher says, *It's why you're in here.*

I'm lying on the bed. His eyes are framed by the hatch.

I say, *Is he here?*

Basher says, *Who?*

I say, *Don't be a cunt. The bastard who killed my mum.*

Basher's face is granite. *Show some fucking respect. In here you call me 'boss'.*

I say, *Respect? For you? I've read my books. In the twenty years after the war you and the Americans killed six million people between you – not soldiers – people. Like me. So you can all fuck off!*

Basher says, *Bulldog was here. He died two years ago. Hung himself. No one tell you in that car park you was living in?*

Bang. Hatch.

Gone.

34.

An hour later it comes to me.

Locked behind iron doors. Secured by a gang of armed men. On the edge of a marsh in the middle of nowhere...

I'm Free At Last.

I'm going to cry. I think. Am I? I don't even know. Wait. No. I'm laughing.

I go to the window and stare out into the dark.

I think, *They can't keep me forever. I'll get out one day and find Martha and say I'm sorry. And maybe one of The Lost Girls will still like me. Even though I look like this and I've done all them bad things. I'll get a job. Turn things round.*

And I'm laughing now because I know that's bollocks.

Then I realise it's not me laughing and I turn round and he's there. Looking like the bastard he always was.

Tattoo on one arm, scar on the other.

He says, *Why are you talking to yourself?*

I say *I'm not.*

He says, *Aren't you?*

I say, *Are you haunting me now?*

He says, *I've haunted you from day fucking one.*

I say, *You can't touch me now though.*

He says, *Can't I?*

I say, *What do you want?*

He says, *You know what I want.*

I say, *You're a murdering bastard.*

He says, <u>*You're*</u> *a murdering bastard.*

I say, *I was drunk.*

He says, *I was drunk. Me and her were always drunk. It's what we did to get away from each other. From the world I made for us.*

I say, *You were a murdering bastard before you killed Mum. Basher showed me the photos.*

He says, *That was nothing. In Kenya I cut a man's balls off and made him eat them. In Malaya I burned a village and killed everyone in it. In Oman I beat a boy to death in front of his mother. It's a matter of record if anyone wants to know but they don't because this whole thing is built on killing.*

I say, *Why didn't you stop it?*

He says, *Why didn't you stop yourself? Why don't all these nice people stop themselves living like they do when they know what it costs?*

I say, *I don't know.*

He says, *It's a mystery.*

I say, *You can go now.*

He says, *I can't do that. Without me you're nothing, none of you. You'd have nothing.*

I say, *I've got three sachets of sugar, a packet of Golden Virginia and some scratchy blankets.*

He says, *You didn't do too well out of it did you, son. But even your lovely drugs come from me.*

I say, *Thanks for the heroin. It helps me sleep.*

He says, *It's time, son.*

I say, *I could've stopped you.*

He says, *I was too strong for you.*

I say, *I had a chance.*

He says, *Why didn't you take it then?*

I say, *I can't remember.*

He says, *I've been waiting for you.*

And we look at each other England to England.

(*The dad opens his arms lovingly.*)

He says, *cammere…*

35.

I'm in the lock-up under the ripped tarpaulins where I've been for two days and two nights.

There's shadows on the door. I peer through the cracks.

Mum is on the ground. Dad is hunched over her in the dark and her legs are kicking out.

Then they stop.

I hear his steps on the gravel.

He unlocks the door and comes in.

The lump hammer's in my hand but I'm scared I'll really hurt him – then what'll happen to me…?

Writing the End of Empire
Ed Edwards

When I first became aware of the horrors of capitalism and the brutal role the British state played in creating and maintaining the system worldwide, I started to hate films about Britain's evil colonial past. Whatever the crimes and/or prejudices portrayed in such films – see *Passage to India*, *Gandhi*, etc. – they always seemed to come with a secret message:

'Look how cruel we were back in the days of Empire, aren't we so much more enlightened now?'

As a left dramatist I was desperate to avoid the same mistake in my own work. But the more I learned about Britain's vampiric past, the more I realised there are problems for writers creating stories at the End of Empire – i.e. about the present.

The more I looked, the more I discovered that the Empire has only really changed its clothes and leaders – slipped on a cloak of invisibility – but underneath the shiny modernity, the decaying and parasitic beast that used to be called Empire, is alive and still kicking. Just hidden.

So, as a dramatist who has to create realistic characters in these circumstances, I have questions:

(i) How much has the *character* of the people who live at the End of Empire really changed since the days of Actual Empire? And,

(ii) What does this mean for writers who want to create realistic characters at the End of Empire?

On the plus side for dramatists, writing 'character' mostly means writing what our protagonists do and say. So pretty much if you can identify that, you've nailed it.

In other words, rather than trying to grasp ever mysterious and illusive psychological characteristics to determine *character* – desire, libido, ego, instinct, the death drive, etc. – dramatists can pretty much say, 'This is what they did, and this is what they said.' Easy.

The tricky part of writing character is *context*. Which changes everything.

For example, the *character* of two lovers in a street staring into each other's eyes and then kissing passionately looks very different if we 'pull back to reveal' people being hanged from a makeshift gallows nearby, operated by our lovers' mates.

But what if the victims of the hanging are fascists who have murdered all of our lovers' friends and family?

Or the hanging is happening in the next street, the victims are innocent, and our lovers are unaware it is happening at all because they are so obsessed with kissing each other? What if we then realise our lovers know what's happening in the next street, but don't really care because they only believe in love?

Or our lovers are under armed guard, they know damn well it's happening in the next street and that they are next? Or, after the kiss, our lovers pull out guns and set off to rescue the innocent victims of the hangings in the next street with a cry of 'Freedom or death!' In each case we feel differently about our lovers and their kiss. In each dramatic vignette they are different characters.

You get the point.

But what if the *writer of the scene* doesn't know there are hangings in the next street and is only interested in our characters and their kiss?

That's when context gets complex, it's easy to mess up and it all gets very postmodern.

So in order to answer my questions I need some proper context.

I need to give a brief account of the British Empire and what became of it. Then ask questions about writing drama in that context.

Two acts. Empire. End of Empire.

This will be ridiculously inadequate as history, but dramatists are allowed to do this shit and call it a provocation. Plus there are loads of notes for fact-checking and further reading if you want to know more, or don't believe me.

Oh, and the original idea for *England & Son* was: *a horror story in which all the horrors are real*. What follows is a horror story in which all the horrors are real.

Fetch the garlic.

Act 1: Empire

Concerning Violence

A month after the Nazi invasion of the Soviet Union in 1941, Hitler declared, 'What India was for England, the territories of Russia will be for us.'[1]

Unfortunately for the world, though, a century beforehand, when the British carried out their robbery and slaughter in India, there was no Soviet Red Army to drive them out and crush them like the beasts they were.

Writing about British violence in India at the time of Empire, Karl Marx described the capitalist class of his day as travelling 'from its home, where it assumes respectable forms, to the colonies, where it goes naked'.[2] That they did. So if you don't like nudity, look away now.

A few years after Marx's remark, in 1857, when Queen Victoria's Empire was nearing its height after a hundred years of robbery and violence by the private armies of the East India Company, poorly armed Indians known as sepoys – actually Indian soldiers used by the British to force their will on India – launched a rebellion to liberate India from British domination. In response, the British behaved like the Nazis in Eastern Europe during World War II.

Following imperial orders, Colonel James Neill – a devout Christian and British army officer – instituted a reign of terror against the civilian population in the vicinity of the Sepoy

Mutiny. At least six thousand men, women and children were killed pretty much straight away. Local British volunteers set up 'hanging parties' and lynched hundreds, including children.

Colonel Neill then sent his soldiers to destroy all the villages in the neighbouring district. 'Slaughter all the men, take no prisoners' were the orders. The soldiers were to make a particular example of the town of Fatehpur with 'all in it to be killed'.[3] A horrified witness suggested that women who refused to leave their burning houses met a kinder fate than other women who were 'ravished to death' by British soldiers.[4]

Following similar gut-wrenching scenes throughout the whole of India, the final stronghold of the sepoy rebellion – the city of Delhi – was destroyed utterly by the British army, alongside many other towns and ancient cities. Thousands of buildings were set alight with families still inside. Tens of thousands of villagers were murdered. Homes and cattle in adjoining districts were destroyed, whole populations were driven out of their ancient homelands to live and die in destitution. There were mass hangings, mass incidents of murderous rape and public torture. Thousands of prisoners were killed horribly, many of them loaded into big guns and fired from them.[5] And that was just the start.

Shortly after the Indian rebellion began, a shocking story about a massacre of surrendered British women and children by Indians was circulated, causing widespread revulsion among whites. Back in Britain, Charles Dickens himself declared a longing for 'the opportunity to exterminate the race (of Indians) upon whom the stain of the late cruelties rested... To blot (the Indian race) out of mankind and raze it off the face of the Earth.'[6] The former Governor General of India called in the House of Lords for every man in Delhi to be castrated and for the city to be renamed 'Eunuchabad'.[7]

But as with similar media tricks today, the details were distorted. The massacre of a few tens of British civilians actually happened *after* the India-wide murderous rampage by the British had already begun – epitomised by good Christian Colonel Neill's expeditions of extermination. Plus, in any event, the murders were carried out by the henchmen of a local prince, previously a collaborator with British rule, who had belatedly joined the revolt and who fully expected to be massacred themselves by British troops who were on their way to do just that.[8]

Recent research by the Indian historian Amaresh Misra suggests in the decade after the 1857 rebellion, the slaughter of Indians ran to as many as ten million men, women and children, as the British launched what was effectively a genocidal war after Queen Victoria's army took over direct rule from the mercenaries of the East India Company.[9]

The orgy of British violence sparked by the Indian Great Rebellion of 1857 did not spring from nowhere. Such gruesome violence had been commonplace in India for the previous hundred years where any hint of rebellion was put down with maximum cruelty as an example to others.

The British behaved as brutally in China, Arabia and northeast Africa as they did in India,[10] where again the figures rival or even dwarf the Nazi rampage in Eastern Europe a hundred years later.

And of course, the bloody conquests of India and China happened at the same time as the development of the plantations in the West Indies, where every torture was used to eke more work out of slaves transported from Africa, or to deter slave rebellions, or put down rebellions once they occurred – which they did with increasing frequency throughout the period.

Such slave revolts – usually very much less violent than their suppression – were inspired at least in part by the Abolitionist Movement among the English working class, who were themselves at that moment organised in revolt against the brutalities of the factory system centred on Manchester.[11] The English factory system itself was only made possible by the seed capital, earned through slavery and colonial plunder, then reinvested into machinery and industrial infrastructure on a scale never before seen in human history.

As slaves on British plantations lost their fear of death and became ever more determined to strike for freedom, so the brutalities inflicted on them reached ever lower depths of cruelty. The British politician and supporter of slavery, Bryan Edwards, captured this duality of cruelty and defiance when he described seeing a risen Jamaican slave punished by fire. The slave was held down and his legs were burned to ashes while he 'uttered not a groan' and somehow 'snatched a brand from the fire that was consuming him and flung it in the face of the executioner'.[12]

It was this emergence of capital out of the profits of slavery, violence, colonial plunder and the brutalities of the early factory system in England that Karl Marx was referring to when he famously wrote that capitalism 'comes into the world… dripping from head to toe, from every pore, with blood and dirt'.[13]

The British slave owners, who in the face of increasing revolts eventually and reluctantly 'gave up' slavery, were massively compensated for their financial losses by the British state. The last payments of this vast booty – as the comedian and activist Mark Thomas pointed out in his recent show *50 Things About Us* – were only made in 2015.

The slaves got nothing.

Can someone please research who exactly received these payments, where they live and organise demonstrations outside their houses until they agree to pay back every penny with two hundred years of interest?

Cheques payable to whom? Discuss.

Oh, and don't forget if you are going to carry out a protest in Britain today you must inform the police who have the right to dictate where you protest, how many people can attend, the form it must take and whether you can make any noise. If you defy them you could face a jail sentence and/or unlimited fines.[14]

Such historic violence by the British Empire was repeated in Asia, Arabia and Africa over approximately three hundred years of Empire from roughly the 1750s to the 1960s. The more the resistance, the greater the British violence.

It's worth ending these notes concerning violence with a recognition that most of the history of this violence is ignored by the majority of historians of Empire. As the anti-colonial writer and professor John Newsinger remarks: 'It is a hidden history... Book after book remains silent on the subject.'[15] Surely one of the most vile of these non-histories is Niall Ferguson's 2003 book *Empire: How Britain Made the Modern World*, which regurgitates for the modern audience all the clichés that the colonised benefitted from being colonised despite some inevitable cruelty.[16] The book helped make Fergusson $80 million by the age of fifty-four.

This gaslighting about Empire is about what happened a hundred and fifty years ago. No wonder what happens at the End of Empire – in our own time – is so hard to discern.

Concerning Economics

In terms of human tragedy, arguably the most destructive violence of the British Empire was economic. The misery and death caused by the economic exploitation of a fifth of the world's population by one class of one small nation off the coast of continental Europe – through rent and mineral extraction, tributary taxation, slavery, unfair trade, financial swindling and downright robbery – was worse than the horrors used to enforce it all.

Take the fate of poor Mr Duffy who lay dying of starvation in his freezing dwelling during the Irish famine of the mid-1840s, obviously unable to pay his rent. His landlord, one Mr Walsh, like hundreds – perhaps thousands – of his fellow landlords at the time, used the famine as an opportunity to clear the land of poor tenants whose families had lived there for generations but who were now too broke to pay decent rents. The Sheriff whose duty it was to execute the eviction, seeing the desperate state of Mr Duffy, hesitated to enforce the order. But, as the parish priest reported later, the landlord '... was inexorable. Duffy was brought out and laid under a shed... once used as a pig cabin and his house (was) thrown down. The landlord, not deeming the possession complete while the pig cabin remained entire, ordered the roof to be removed and poor Duffy, having no friend to shelter him, remained under the open air for two days and two nights, until death put an end to him.'[17]

The so-called Potato Famine killed a million Irish people while, at a conservative estimate, enough food was exported to England to feed the population of Ireland three times over.[18] The Prime Minister of England was himself an evicting landlord. Henry Temple, 3rd Viscount Palmerston had two thousand of his own starving Irish tenants deported to Canada promising publicly to pay each of them £2 to £5 pounds on arrival. But at the other end no one turned up with the money.[19]

Naturally such evictions provoked the murder of some landlords, including one Major Denis Mahon of County Roscommon, who had paid passage for some five hundred of his tenets on a 'coffin ship', as such vessels were known. Over 150 of Mahon's emigrants were dead by the time the vessel docked in Canada and most of the survivors subsequently died too. Mahon was, of course, celebrated in the British press as a humane landlord cut down by a murderous assassin urged on by the parish priest.[20]

Such was the economic plight of the Irish whose land was emptied many times over by individual economic miseries heaped on it over two centuries by the Empire. At one million dead over a few years, the famine was only the most cataclysmic and collective low point.

Now zoom out and multiply by thirty to fifty.

By the 1870s – the year the 'scramble for Africa' began in earnest – two hundred years of colonial economic disruption in India and China had destroyed utterly the traditional village economies with their ancient safeguards against disease and famine, replacing them with nothing of use to the indigenous populations. So, when the great droughts of the period struck in 1876 and again in 1899, accompanied by hugely destructive epidemics of malaria, bubonic plague, dysentery, smallpox and cholera, the results were cataclysmic. It is estimated by the most recent research that a staggering thirty to fifty million Indians and Chinese died of disease and starvation while British administrators and Empire soldiers fought only to protect the recently established free-market mechanisms and only used the opportunity to strengthen their hold on the countries' economies.[21]

In the 1800s, the Indian cotton industry was destroyed by cheap cotton imports from Manchester, throwing millions into destitution. Opium grown in India helped bring China to its economic knees and created the greatest opium epidemic in history. It also helped England balance its international payments for tea which before the opium wars was draining Britain of gold and silver.[22] The profits of the opium trade also paid for the upkeep of the British government of India.[23] Over the period of British domination, India's domestic share of world trade plummeted from 25% to 2%.[24]

By 1870, Britain faced fierce competition from other European and US capitalists who wanted in on the game. These powers concentrated industrial manufacture in their own countries and took what they needed from their colonies to feed the vast machinery of wealth creation.[25] The super-profits earned in the colonies by Europeans enabled the Industrial Revolution to really take off and transform the Empire heartlands into the commodity-and-infrastructure rich world we know today – while the rest of the world went to shit.[26]

Concerning Character

There are huge and important questions about who has the right – or who does not have the right – to tell the story of the colonial oppressed. But here I'm really talking about creating Western characters in Western drama. The rest is context.

So, what of the character of the early capitalist class who did all the raping and killing and living off the proceeds?

At the height of their extravagant, worldwide orgy of exploitation, swindling, robbery, rape and other violence, did these grotesque beings walk around growling like demons, dripping blood from their talons, biting the heads off babies on the streets of London, Bristol, Liverpool and Manchester?

In fact, they were the most respected, venerated, fashionably dressed and publicly minded gentlemen of their age. They had great manners. Many were writers, poets and sponsors of public works. They were devout church and theatregoers and a good catch for a potential wife.

Take Captain Wentworth in Jane Austen's *Persuasion*.

We're told Wentworth came back from sea in 1817 with a cool £2.2 million quid in today's money. He is supposed to have made this in a few short years in what is vaguely described as 'prize money'. But come on. Even if he made all that by chasing bad guys – like pirates and illegal slave traders – how did the majority of men his age on those there high seas come into that kind of cash? Best not to ask, like the rest of the characters in the book.

But Wentworth is probably still a fair representation of the dreamboat of his day. Rich, witty and gallant. Glad to have done his duty. In his backstory he's not allowed to marry the heroine of the tale when he's young because he doesn't have the dosh. But then when he makes his fortune at sea he comes back to claim his female booty. The big climax of the drama in the novel isn't the dirty stuff of early Empire; it's our heroine giddily falling off a wall to bang her head and be rescued by our devoted hero.

It's a really enjoyable read even if it sidesteps the great drama of the day in terms of context. It's a genuine insight into how the people who ran the early Empire experienced each other, how they saw themselves. They were obviously nice people.

Who needs context really, eh?

Empire officers carrying out the actual torture and slaughter on the ground, were very often religious. One such man claimed he saw 'the finger of God in this', meaning the mass slaughter and mistreatment of Indians in the 1870s.[27]

Good old Colonel James Neill – who took his troops raping and killing, and whose men killed everyone in Fatehpur (and raped the women) – wrote: 'God grant I may have acted with Justice. I know I have with severity, but under the circumstances I trust for forgiveness.'[28] I think he meant the forgiveness of God not his Indian victims. Happily Colonel Neill was shot dead before the end of the rebellion at Lucknow. The loyal officer was, however, awarded a posthumous knighthood by Queen Victoria.[29] We don't know what happened at the Pearly Gates.

Queen Victoria herself was kept informed of the degree and nature of the slaughter in India by one of her more sensitive officers who was disturbed by the horrors he had personally witnessed. The officer became a laughing stock.[30] Queen Victoria did nothing to stop the rampage, only – as we've seen – ordering her troops to take over control of India from the mercenaries of the East India Company as the Great Rebellion was put down.[31] After this, as we've seen, the murder continued for a decade.[32] When the dust finally settled, British Prime Minister Gladstone had his bejewelled queen declared 'Empress of India'.

So how does a dramatist realistically depict a character who apparently genuinely believes they are acting for God, but also orders the mass rape and killing of thousands, or even tens of thousands of civilians?

Simple. We say what they did and what they said, but for God's sake put it in context. Give the facts. But there's the rub. Facts don't fit well into drama. They just don't. If you even actually know them.

Hence this essay.

And what of Dickens's character? The good bloke of Victorian literature. Of course, he was duped by a clever propaganda trick, but wasn't the plight of Victorian street kids also grossly misrepresented in the press? Not to mention the whole of the rest of the poor in Victorian England? Dickens apparently saw through all that, writing poignantly about them and their predicaments. Maybe he was just 'old-fashioned' when it came to race? Or was India too far away for him to realise?

The English revolutionary Ernest Jones wasn't old-fashioned about the humanity of the Indian race. He knew exactly what was going on all those thousands of miles away, and he stood by and spoke up for the Indian rebels at every opportunity.[33] As did Marx and Engels.

Stupid Charles.

Great writer, though.

And what of the character of the English working class at the time of Empire?

During the early Industrial Revolution, the newly formed and horribly exploited British working class were staunch supporters of the Abolition Movement and an inspiration to risen slaves throughout the Caribbean.[34]

The early 1800s saw a powerful working-class movement emerge in the face of the Peterloo Massacre to become the revolutionary Chartist Movement of the 1840s – centred on the demand 'One Man One Vote'.[35]

At the time of the Chartists' campaign, their demand was a revolutionary one because the working class were the vast majority and, at the time, real power did actually reside in the British Parliament. A fact that would change as soon as the vote was expanded.[36] As Karl Marx recognised, one vote per worker would at that moment have made an instant ruling class out of the working class. And if once they had seized power, male workers included women in the vote, as surely they would, it would have massively strengthened their majority.

The capitalists were having none of it, of course, and gave the English working class a taste of colonial-style violence, with hangings of political leaders and massacres of unarmed protesters. Limited in scale compared to the violence in India, China and the rest, the violence was nonetheless ferocious when it came, with for example twenty-two shot dead in Newport,

Wales, in December 1839.[37] Much of the violence was blamed
on the Chartists themselves, as is often the case when the shit
hits the fan.[38] But the violence worked, by terrifying more
respectable elements of the Chartist Movement, and threatening
the unity.

When in 1848 a petition was finally delivered to Parliament
demanding one man one vote, signed by one-and-a-half million,
it was rejected out of hand. The resulting disturbances were used
as an excuse to launch an all-out assault on the Chartists, which
caused the respectable elements to finally abandon it. By 1858,
the Chartist Movement had shrivelled to a handful of hopefuls.

But even in the 1860s, during the US Civil War, the bulk of
the working class in Manchester still underwent incredible
hardships rather than work the cotton imported from the
Southern slave states in the famous 'cotton strikes'.[39] Though by
the time of the Fenian uprising in Ireland only two years later,
the English working class seemed to have lost something of
their stomach for international solidarity and failed to prevent
the execution of five innocent Irishmen in Manchester, who
were falsely accused of killing a prison guard when trying to
rescue Fenian leaders from custody.

Instead, ten thousand people turned up to watch them hang.[40]

After the defeat of the Chartists, the more skilled industrial
workers in England began to act more in their own individual
interests and organised themselves into the first legal trade
unions. These unions were designed to keep other workers
out of the best-paid work and drive up the wages of their own
members. This was the origin of the trade union movement in
Britain.[41]

With honourable exceptions, by the start of World War I in
1914, the majority of the better off European and US workers
in the industrial heartlands had largely turned their back on
revolutionary internationalism, and had settled down to try and
get the best deal for themselves out of a capitalist system that
was a vampiric beast sucking the blood from whole of the rest
of the world.[42]

Act 2: The End of Empire

Luckily for the world, after World War II, the British realised how, during the Empire, there'd been instances of bad behaviour and racism, some of it shocking. So, despite their better judgement – and, yes, sometimes reluctantly – the British granted independence to the former Empire and went it alone.

More often than not, the newly independent countries of the former Empire made a mess of governing themselves. But the British – with help from their good friends, the Americans – kept forces stationed all over the world for just such an eventuality.

If things got too far out of hand, the British could – and still do – intervene to save their former subjects from themselves and from each other – and especially from other dark forces such as Chinese Dictators, Bloodthirsty Russians, or Assorted Religious Fanatics who oppress women and LGBTQ+ people.

This mission to save the world from itself is a great responsibility that can involve the British in tricky moral and political dilemmas. But we're determined to see decency and democracy maintained the world over. We're good like that. It's who we are and who we've always been underneath it all.

Some version or other of this myth is propagated 24/7 in the West – with big results. Huge swathes of Westerners believe it, or something like it, with adjustments for political creed. Even some socialists. In other words, most Westerners believe that the end of the colonial period meant the end of imperialism. Imperialism being the political and/or economic domination of smaller or weaker countries by powerful ones for the benefit of the powerful ones.

What really happened?

Concerning Violence II

The end of the Empire was a bloodbath.

After World War II, hundreds of millions of people in the colonies across Africa and Asia rose up to free themselves from

European rule. The rebellions were inspired in part by Western anti-fascist slogans, partly by the Soviet Red Army's stunning victories against Nazism in Europe, but mostly by their own brutal oppression at the hands of Europeans.

The scale and ferocity of the West's murderous response to this worldwide rebellion – a response led by Britain, France and the US – was as horrific as in the days of Empire.

Take Kenya.

In the early 1900s, the Kikuyu people, numbering two-or-so million souls had the misfortune to live on the best land in Kenya when white settlers came to claim the land on behalf of the British Empire. Many of the later settlers had fought in World War I. The newly arrived whites were terrible farmers and bad workers, and had it not been for the Empire sustaining them with grants and preferable terms of trade they would have failed.[43]

Gradually, though, with great brutality and ruthless legal trickery, the white settlers rid the best land of the Kikuyu people and, with the help of the boundless cheap labour of the ruined Kikuyu, eventually established vastly profitable plantations growing mainly, but not only, coffee.[44]

The majority of the Kikuyu were driven into reservations on the poorest land which couldn't possibly sustain their numbers. Here they starved and fought among themselves, or fell ill. The rest found refuge in the slums of the sweltering and disease-ridden capital city, Nairobi. The lucky ones established desperately poor farms on inadequate plots of land near the white settlers, where they were bullied and used as cheap labour on the adjoining plantations, living in constant fear of eviction or being swindled out of their possession.[45]

Over fifty years or so, the Kikuyu people went from being among the most blessed tribal people of the world to the most wretched.

Those few Kikuyu who managed to get an education pleaded the case of their desperate people again and again to the various branches of the colonial government – and even to the British in

Britain. They met with indifference and contempt at every turn, sometimes imprisonment.[46]

By 1952, the Kikuyu people had formed the Kenya Land and Freedom Army and launched an uprising against colonial rule.

The colonial government's response, backed by the British army, is among the most brutal and shameful episodes of human history. When it was over, the British government destroyed most of the papers documenting their behaviour,[47] but research by the Pulitzer Prize-winning Harvard historian Caroline Elkins has recently uncovered the truth. If anyone had spoken to the Kikuyu survivors before this they could have easily discovered the truth a lot earlier. But this is how history is done.

To break the staunch solidarity of the Kikuyu people, British Crown forces established a vast system of concentration camps, at first for men, but when the British discovered the backbone of Kikuyu solidarity was the women, for tens of thousands of women also.[48]

Supporters of the rebel Land and Freedom Army took an oath of allegiance to the cause based on the traditional tribal system. Almost all the Kikuyu people took it.[49] The oath was sacrosanct and a matter of great seriousness. To break the oath was to abandon yourself and your people. The aim of the colonial violence was twofold. Destroy the Land and Freedom Army. Break Kikuyu civilian solidarity.

Through systematic torture, civilians would be made to individually 'confess' their oath and declare allegiance to the colonial authorities. Those who did confess could become 'loyalists' and be granted small privileges. Those who did not were to be destroyed spiritually, culturally and physically.[50]

As the war intensified, so the main privilege on offer to loyalists could only really be to escape being beaten, or worked and tortured to death in the concentration camps.

And to become a loyalist, prisoners would have to prove themselves by beating former comrades to death, or inflicting terrible torture on them, or by becoming camp guards.

Converted loyalists were often the most brutal. The right to inflict such suffering on powerless inmates in turn became one of the few privileges of confession.

And, of course, once women were introduced into the system, rape and sexual torture became loyalist privileges too.

The violence against prisoners was carried out by settlers, British district officers, the Kenyan police force, African loyalists, and members of the British army. Bottles (often broken), gun barrels, knives, snakes, vermin and hot eggs were thrust up men's rectums and women's vaginas. Women's breasts were squeezed with pliers. Male prisoners were castrated and made to eat their own testicles. Prisoners would be beaten to death in front of other prisoners. Prisoners were butchered to death slowly with knives. Prisoners were publicly strung up and had sand stuffed into their anuses, often until their guts ruptured and they died. Prisoners were dragged to death behind Land Rovers, had their fingers cut off, were made to watch executions and then told to dig their own graves. Prisoners were burnt alive.[51] Many white settlers frankly and sincerely expressed the view that the only 'solution' was the extermination of the entire Kikuyu race.[52]

Tens of thousands of prisoners were purposefully worked to death in the sweltering heat with water and food restricted. Anyone slacking could be beaten to death on the spot. Their comrades were made to bury them. Groups of those who refused to confess were taken out, made to dig their own graves and shot *en masse*.[53]

Women prisoners were subjected to endless sexual torture. One women survivor reported being taken with a large group of other 'hardcore' women – as those who refused to confess were called – to be shot. After the group had been made to dig their own mass grave, the survivor was selected by an officer to be spared. She was instead kept as a sex slave.[54]

The British governor of the whole colony of Kenya – one Evelyn Baring – of Barings Bank fame – would, on receiving complaints of sexual violence, come to inspect the women's camps. He is reported to have stood and stared at the women as they squatted before him, caked in filth, while the good governor again and again found nothing untoward.[55]

The majority of the Kikuyu population passed through this system at some point during the rebellion. The entire Kikuyu population of Nairobi was rounded up in one day and poured into the camps. Most who escaped the official concentration camps – mainly women, children and the elderly – met a terrible fate themselves in the parallel 'protected village' system that was designed also to receive people released from the concentration camps.[56]

To cut the Land and Freedom Army off from their Kikuyu supporters, the British forced a huge proportion of the Kikuyu people out of their existing homes and settlements into these villages.[57] The system was a model developed by the British during their war against the Malayan people, which was (and still is) considered a model of counter-revolutionary success by the British military establishment.[58]

In Kenya, the protected village campaign was carried out in a hurricane of violence. The traditional villages were burned and the women, children and elderly were driven into new homes. Many were killed on the spot to terrify the rest into submission.[59]

When they arrived at the protected villages, the destitute Kikuyu people found nothing but a cordon of soldiers and armed loyalists. There was no shelter, no water, or sanitation facilities, or medical supplies. Food was a thin gruel. Then there was a regime of brutal forced labour as the villagers built their own village, chased by loyalists with clubs and whips. There were rapes and random killings of villagers, including children. Thousands died of disease and exhaustion.[60]

The loyalists lived nearby in comparative luxury, in huts built by the forced labourers. Loyalist wives did no forced labour.[61]

It is estimated that three hundred thousand Kikuyu people out of a population of one-and-a-half million died under these savage conditions of murder and forced labour.[62] Equivalent in Britain to approximately seven-and-a-half million dead.

It's worth saying clearly, out loud. Forced labour is slavery. This is 1954-6, in Kenya, overseen by British Crown forces with Queen Elizabeth II of England at their head. A queen whose image, by the way, was everywhere in the camps and protected villages, whose anthem was sung loudly during murders and tortures, especially by groups of white settlers.[63] The aim of much of the forced labour was to work people to death as a form of political terror.

Eventually, isolated from the majority of their people, the Kikuyu people's Land and Freedom Army, though fearsome, brave and well organised, was certain to be defeated. The white terror worked. The mass of the Kikuyu people had 'confessed' or been driven from their land and homes, murdered, or worked to death. Only the tiniest 'hardcore' remained who refused to break.[64]

The military task complete, the British officially withdrew from Kenya, leaving behind a vulnerable and corrupt political structure built entirely out of the loyalist community and those prepared to work with them.[65]

By now, the loyalists were up to their necks in a sea of blood. Tens of thousands were guilty of crimes against humanity for which they could be held accountable if they weren't very careful. They were living in stolen property, on stolen land, on borrowed time. They were vulnerable to their own people who would hate them forever, and they were vicious as hell.

The son of the first president of independent Kenya, Peter Muigai Kenyatta, with the full knowledge of his father, took part in the notorious interrogation regime, during the terror.[66] Another of his sons, Uhuru Kenyatta, was president from 2013 to 2022. In the years after World War II, each colonial rebellion was different, but what happened in Kenya was typical. In most cases, ruthless violence was used by the former colonial powers to weaken or destroy revolutionary movements and sculpt Western-friendly gangster regimes. Only then was power handed over. These newly formed elites were totally dependent on the West for political support, arms and, most of all, a market for their crops and minerals.[67]

Welcome to the End of Empire.

Concerning Economics II

Before he died, Fidel Castrol urged progressives and revolutionaries the world over to study economics.

This is a big ask because – in all seriousness – Western economists themselves don't seem to understand economics. So when the 2008 banking crisis hit, students at Manchester University asked their lecturers to explain it – and famously they couldn't.[68]

Modern economics is complicated by design and often shrouded in secrecy. The most expensively educated people in the world are engaged in making it so. University economics curriculums have given up teaching economic history and Marxist theories, instead focussing on statistical analysis of market mechanisms, and training students for roles at investment banks or for life in the boardrooms of multinational corporations.[69]

Meanwhile, in the real world, economists and lawyers employed by multinational corporations, backed by Western governments, have created a wicked web of complicated economic mechanisms by which the West continues to enrich itself at the expense of the former colonies.

Example.

Prepare for a brain bleed.

But bear with me cos this shit is important and complexity is part of the method.

Take, Investor-State Dispute Settlement (ISDS) courts. I can hear you yawning already. But these mothers are *mean*! You can admire them like you might the claws of a lion or the talons of an eagle.

ISDS courts are nasty legal entities designed to stop countries like Kenya acting in their own interests instead of in the interests of the corporations of the former mother country. Even in a thoroughly corrupted country like Kenya, this could sometimes happen as a regime tries to win votes, or a dictator tries to justify their position. Or make a quick buck.

These courts are essentially kangaroo courts inside the World Bank.[70] They were set up in the 1960s as the liberation movements in the colonies reached their climax, in order to protect Western corporate interests in the affected countries.[71]

Cases are heard in Washington or The Hague. Many of the judges (called arbitrators) are former members of US government administrations, or other such characters.[72]

To get help from the World Bank, governments must sign up to the jurisdiction of these courts – though calling them courts is generous, implying a degree of fairness or a potential for justice that just isn't there. The judgements of these bodies are legally binding. If a country refuses to accept a judgement, its assets, including shipping, goods, money, bonds or gold held in US or European banks can be seized.[73]

In these courts the world's largest corporations, employing the world's most expensively trained lawyers, can sue the world's smallest and most vulnerable countries for billions of dollars for threatening their profitability, or for interfering in their business activities. Such a threat to business can be, for instance – and this is a common one – a small country demanding environmental protections before issuing a drilling licence.

At the time of writing, Honduras is being sued for $11 billion by an international corporation for not allowing the establishment of a special economic zone on its territory. Special economic zones have their own security forces, their own tax laws, and are exempt from national employment laws. In other words, they are mini-colonies.

The total gross national income for the whole of Honduras is approximately $29 billion. So the corporation is suing Honduras for more than a third of its entire annual income.[74]

Conversely, the world's largest corporations can have the rulings of the supreme courts of small countries overturned in these tribunals.

So, for example, Ecuador's highest court ordered Texaco (now taken over by Chevron) to pay $9 billion in compensation, after it was revealed the company had pumped billions of litres of carcinogenic toxins into the environment. Indigenous Ecuadorians reported Texaco's oil workers dynamiting their homes and subjecting them to sexual and other violence.[75]

The ruling by Ecuador's highest court demanding compensation from Texaco/Chevron was overturned by the World Bank's court.[76]

There are many other such secretive, invisible and nasty legal instruments out there, such as Bilateral Trade Agreements (BTAs). Again with BTAs, the complexity – hidden in the small print – plays an important role. So people signing BTAs in the small nations are often unaware of the real implications, which are only revealed later, when the small countries are suddenly hit by vast lawsuits overseen by the ISDS courts.When he was released from jail, Nelson Mandela toured the world and was asked to sign a blizzard of BTAs by Western businessmen and diplomats to signal his return to the international fold. Mandela signed and as a result South Africa is now tied up in endless nasty legal cases. The nation's hands are cuffed in new chains when it comes to crafting its own economic future.[77]

In other words, highly secretive and specialist kangaroo courts whose deciding vote is held by a Westerner have more power than the highest courts in the countries of the former colonies.[78]

There are thousands of such lawsuits now underway the world over. And there has been an exponential growth in such cases since the end of the USSR, since which time smaller countries have had nowhere else to turn for their trade.[79]

You get the idea.

Despite the supposed End of Empire, the West employs a million economic mechanisms to exploit the rest of the world for the benefit of its own populations who, relative to the rest of the world, are sitting pretty.

The main weapon is, of course, the boundless and infinitely exploitable pool of cheap labour, the exploitation of which has, since the end of Empire, been massively expanded and intensified, especially since jobs from the West are being exported there.[80]

Check the label on your shirt or trousers (not the washing instructions).

In his seminal work *How Europe Under Developed Africa*, the African revolutionary writer and activist Walter Rodney suggests that if we compare a map of Europe to a map of Africa, even a quick glance reveals a deep truth about modern imperial exploitation. In Europe, the roads are thick lines connecting the major cities to one another. In the former colonies, all roads lead to the sea[81].

We've already seen how the industrial systems of the West emerged (dripping blood from every pore) from the exploitation of slaves and the colonial people of the world. I'm arguing here that the imperial system continues to this day, though disguised – and that, without it, the West would have to change utterly, head to toe.[82]

Here are three final stats before we return to the question of portraying Western characters in drama:

1. If the people of the colonial world were currently paid wages at the same rate as workers in the West, all of the profits made by all the business and enterprises in the West would be wiped out.[83]

2. A person on the poverty line in the US or Europe is still in the top 14% of earners worldwide.[84]

3. A person on the average wage in US or Europe is in the top 4% of earners worldwide.[85]

Concerning Character II

So what of the main characters in this great drama of the vampire north secretly sucking the lifeblood of the global south like a bloated mediaeval aristocrat?

Certainly governments and big business have always had secrets, but for the main driving force of world politics and economics – imperialism – to be something the world has to pretend doesn't exist takes us to a whole new level of deception.

How does a dramatist create realistic characters in *this* context?

Probably the easiest characters to portray are those of the white Kenyan settlers and other racists in the colonial world as the visible Empire comes to an end. These racists invariably describe the Kikuyu as 'savage', 'barbaric', 'primitive', 'brutal', and 'inhuman', then behave in the most savage, barbaric, primitive, brutal and inhuman ways towards the Kikuyu.

Talk about victim-blaming.

In my opening dramatic vignettes, the white settlers are our first lovers kissing when we 'pull back to real' people being hanged nearby. Their actions are easy to judge and to depict. But once the corrupt post-independence regime takes over, white-settler racism has to lower its voice in public and the context changes.

So now in the dramatic vignettes, our lovers are kissing on one street while people are being hanged on the next – or in the next town – or, most likely, in the poorest districts where our lovers have never ventured – by people our lovers can plausibly say are nothing to do with them. How much do they really believe their own story? We don't know. But already it's harder to show them as they really are. It's easier for our lovers – and our audience – to kid themselves, or only to be interested in love.

What about the modern British army in all this?

Is there a change of character from the Victorian soldiers in India with their open and honest rape and slaughter of Indian civilians? Their god-fearing and gentlemanly habits? What do military Brits and other Westerners say and do today?

After World War II, with the defeat first of the French army in Vietnam at the hands of a popular people's army, then the defeat of the US army – the greatest military force in human history – by the same poorly armed but determined force, new methods of Western warfare became imperative. As we've seen, if the Western powers were to maintain their economic dominance they could no longer show their faces directly in the colonies for fear of giving the population an obvious target to mobilise against.

They would have to start lying big time.

The new form of secret warfare became known as 'the dirty war'[86]. So now Western powers would do as little as possible of the hands-on stuff themselves. Instead they would train and secretly arm official and semi-official forces – or very fucking *un*official forces to do their dirty work for them. Such as Mujahidin in Afghanistan (later to become Al-Qaeda) or the brutal drug gangs in Latin American that brought the crack epidemic to the US in the 1980s, and have since brought such chaos to Latin America as a whole.[87]

A member of one such unofficial military force – used by the British to overthrow the government of Libya in 2011 – blew up the Manchester Arena in May 2017, killing twenty-two people and injuring 1,017.[88]

During the 1970s and 1980s, the US military had a notorious facility in Fort Benning, Georgia, known as 'The School of the Americas' (since renamed Fort Moore, but still going strong),[89] where many of the most violent of the Latin American military dictatorships were trained in the art of crushing progressive political movements.[90] The torturers and death squads of El Salvador, Chile, Argentina, Haiti, Uruguay, Brazil, Peru, Bolivia, Honduras, Guatemala and the rest received instruction here and went on a decades-long rampage of kidnapping and killing of Indigenous peoples. Hundreds of thousands of trade unionists, feminists, socialists, communists and Indigenous activists lost their lives in horrific circumstances. Methods included drugging victims and pushing them out of military aircraft over the Pacific Ocean.[91]

The US government, meanwhile, kept its own hands clean and was able to portray itself to the world as the respectable peacemaker, a paragon of liberal democracy. In other words, the President of the USA could go round looking like Queen Victoria. I don't mean the black silk dress.

In Britain we train many of the most notorious post-colonial (Commonwealth) militaries at the Royal Military Academy at Sandhurst, where top honours are sponsored by the states of Kuwait, Qatar and King Hussein of Jordan.

So our contemporary military now say one thing and do entirely another. They too have become slippery and very hard to portray in proper context. But, of course, that's the whole point: disguise or 'plausible deniability', as it's known officially. No doubt our military leaders believe they are doing this for the highest reasons – but nonetheless, they are big fat liars.

Britain's most renown contemporary military strategist – General Frank Kitson – cut his teeth during the genocide in Kenya where he personally began to forge new methods of warfare, including what he calls 'psychological operations'[92]. Which might include, for example, soldiers 'blacking up' and committing outrages that could be blamed on rebels[93].

The British government has now effectively admitted that this general went on to run loyalist death squads during the dirty war in the north of Ireland in the early 1970s. These death squads targeted a range of people in the Catholic community, often civilians.[94] Throughout the whole period of war in Ireland, British Crown forces maintained they were only there as peacekeepers[95]– i.e., keeping warring Catholics and Protestants apart.[96]

The whole British strategy during the war in Ireland was effectively a psychological operation. Otherwise known as a lie.

On 16 March 1988, a loyalist terrorist launched a gun and grenade attack on Catholic mourners – including children – at a funeral in Belfast. This was the funeral of three Irish Republican volunteers who had been executed by British soldiers in Gibraltar after they had already surrendered.[97] The funeral was surrounded by a huge British army security cordon, supposedly to keep the mourners safe. Yet the loyalist terrorist perpetrator somehow got through the security cordon to launch his attack, killing three people, wounding sixty.[98]

So, in our vignettes, our kissing lovers might be British soldiers (uniforms can be sexy, yes?) forming part of a security cordon at this very funeral. They haven't got a clue that their superior officers have concocted a plan to let a loyalist terrorist attack the mourners, but even if they did, our lovers might not care because they will have comrades who have been shot by guerrillas defending the Catholic community that our lovers are fighting, even though they're pretending otherwise.

It's complicated, but still possible to portray – just. To round off our soldiers in Ireland kissing story: it turns out they should have been more careful to hide their kiss, because when there's a political scandal about the leaky security cordon they are court-martialed for kissing when they should have been doing their jobs properly and not accidentally letting a loyalist terrorist bomb a Catholic funeral. This last bit is entirely fictional. There was no real political scandal.

You get the idea.

So what about the rest of us?

Here it starts to become very difficult for a dramatist.

How does a writer realistically portray what we ordinary, everyday Westerners do and say in this messed-up context? Say, someone on the average wage in an average town. Which as we've seen, puts them unknowingly in the top 4% of earners worldwide, even though they might feel skint and miserably insecure.

In world terms, our kissing lovers – wherever in the West they find themselves – are now the most luxurious aristocrats who are nowhere near any hangings or skulduggery at Irish republican funerals!

Our lovers might be average, universally accepted as 'normal', and not require qualification in the West, but in world terms are they not outlandishly strange characters, even grotesque?

Any love story set in Nazi Germany during the build-up
to World War II – before the fighting breaks out and the
concentration camps really get going – automatically becomes
a love story with politics and history somewhere near the very
heart of it. It's impossible or bizarre to portray lovers in these
circumstances without the context. The context automatically
becomes the theme.

A love story set in USA, UK or France during the appalling
and far more widespread campaigns of worldwide political
murder conducted in the soon-to-be-former colonies by these
nations can easily be just a simple love story with no wider
context at all.

It's almost impossible to portray these modern Western lovers in
proper context without the craziest narrative gymnastics. What
even is realism in these circumstances?

Is realism possible in a surreal world?

In Dickens's day, the mass of the downtrodden were in the next
street. Dickens probably had to step over them to get to the
shops. The cities were full of the kind of poverty we only really
see today in the global south. There were public hangings most
weeks down Dickens's way. And he couldn't help being aware
of at least *some* of the real context even if he disconnected it
from the excesses of the Empire in India.

Today our most expensively educated and highly paid
journalists most often seem honestly unaware of the proper
context of their own lives.

Most ordinary Westerners *feel* for the wretched of the Earth, but
few grasp the reality. This can be dangerous, perhaps even fatal
for our collective fate.

Take the epic miners' strike of 1984/5, when two hundred
thousand British coal miners, their entire communities and their
political allies suddenly had to face the might of the British state
head on.

Thatcher's government launched a carefully planned attack
against the National Union of Mineworkers, in order to break

the back of the trade union movement as a whole. But by the time the attack came, the British working-class movement had for decades been insulated from the struggles of the poor in Zimbabwe, Kenya, Malaya, Sri Lanka, Yemen, Ireland and the rest of the former Empire, as the masses there fought heroically – and died in their millions.

The British working class as a whole had not learned the bitter lessons of those struggles and – with honourable exceptions – had done little to intervene in any significant way. So by 1984 – despite the heroism of the mining communities that fought to the bitter end – in world terms, the miners and their allies were relatively easy pickings for the battle-hardened British state.

Engels warned us as far back as 1874 with these words. 'A people which oppresses another cannot emancipate itself.'[99]

So what now? Everyone with a heart knows bitter new struggles are coming. It's in the air. You can feel it.

But because of the nature of the beast, if the capitalists endure, our planet will almost certainly die. Or, even before we get there, we could find ourselves in the midst of a nuclear war centred on Europe.

In this context, I have questions.

In the coming fight, if we Westerners demand from the British, American, or European governments only higher wages, or better health and social services, or a green, sustainable economy, without considering these demands in the post-colonial context – are we in fact only demanding a fairer, more sustainable imperialism?

If so, is this to be paid for by the continued misery and degradation of billions of our brothers and sisters in the global south?

And if so, what sort of characters are we?

And doesn't history show this can only lead to defeat?

Can't we instead try to understand our actions in their proper context and look for a new way forward that doesn't ignore everything that has gone before?

Can't we find a way to fight alongside those who have nothing to lose, as more and more of us lose everything?

I hope so. But I can't say for sure that we will.

I do know I have to try and write about it, though.

Realistically and in context.

Endnotes

1   Adolf Hitler et al., *Hitler's Table Talk*, 1941–1944: His Private
     Conversations (New York: Enigma Books, 2008).

2   Marx, K. *The Future Results of British Rule in India* (London. New York
     Daily Tribune, August 8, 1853), p. 85.

3   Newsinger, J. *The Blood Never Dried: A People's History of the British
     Empire* (London: Bookmarks Publications, 2013) pp. 84-89.

4   Newsinger (2013) p. 89.

5   Newsinger (2013) pp. 84-89.

6   Oddie, W., 'Dickens and the Indian Mutiny', *The Dickensian*, 68 (1972),
     pp. 4–5. Quoted in Newsinger (2013).

7   Newsinger (2013) p. 89.

8   Newsinger (2013) p. 89.

9   Misra, A., (2008) *War of Civilisations: India, AD 1857*. Rupa & Company.
     See also: Ramesh, R., 2007. *India's Secret History: 'A Holocaust, One
     Where Millions Disappeared…'*. *Guardian*. 2007 Aug 24.

10   Newsinger (2013) pp. 56-73.

11   See for instance *Guardian*, 4 Feb 2013, 'Lincoln's great debt to
     Manchester'.

12   Newsinger (2013) p. 27.

13   Karl Marx, (1867). *Capital: A Critique of Political Economy, Volume 1*.
     Progress Publishers, Moscow, USSR.

14   See The Public Order Act 2023.

15   Newsinger (2013).

16   Ferguson, N., 2012. *Empire: How Britain Made the Modern World*.
     Penguin UK.

17   Quoted in Newsinger (2013) p. 47.

18   *The Journal of the Royal Society of Antiquaries of Ireland*. Vol. 82, No. 2
     (1952) pp. 99–108 (10 pages). According to Marx and Engles, the famine
     itself was in large part caused by soil exhaustion fostered by rents so high
     tenant farmers couldn't properly fertilise the land. Marx, K. and Engels, F.,
     Ireland and the Irish Question (Moscow).

19   Newsinger (2013) pp. 46-50.

20   Newsinger (2013) pp. 46-50.

21   Davies, M. *Late Victorian Holocausts*. (London: Verso, 2010), p. 7. For an
      exhaustive study of modern-day practices where Western financial regimes
      use any sort of disaster – such as the 2004 Indian Ocean Tsunami – to prey
      on the weakest people on Earth and strengthen their hold over foreign
      governments, see Klein, N., *The Shock Doctrine: The Rise of Disaster
      Capitalism* (Macmillan, 2007).

22   McCoy, A.W. *The Politics of Heroin: CIA Complicity in the Global
      Drug Trade, Afghanistan, Southeast Asia, Central America* (Chicago, IL:
      Lawrence Hill, 2003).

23   Newsinger (2013) p. 57.

24   Book review: *Shashi Tharoor's Angry History of British Rule in India is a
      Timely Response to Empire Nostalgia. Irish Times*. 4 March 2017.

25   Of the Great Powers Russia was the exception in terms of industrial
      development and was therefore the weakest and most unstable power with
      relatively tiny industrial development in St Petersburg and Moscow only.

26   Zac Cope. *The Wealth of (Some) Nations Divided World Divided Class:
      Global Political Economy and the Stratification of Labour.* (Pluto, 2019).

27   Newsinger (2013) p. 86.

28   Newsinger (2013) p. 85.

29   Newsinger (2023) p. 86.

30   Newsinger (2023) p. 86.

31   Newsinger (2013) p. 91.

32   Misra (2008). Ramesh, R., 2007.

33   Newsinger (2013) p. 90.

34   Newsinger (2013) p. 37.

35   See for example Dan Glazebrook. *The Tragedy of Corbynism*. Counter
      Punch. December 27, 2020.

36   As more and more of the population were included in the national vote
      – which only began after the defeat of the revolutionary Chartists – so
      gradually real power was consciously removed from Parliament. At first to
      the cabinet collectively – but then, by the time the first Labour government
      came to power, the only position left with any real power in the British
      Parliament was the person of the Prime Minister itself. The rest of the
      power was wielded exclusively by Whitehall and the other Crown forces:
      army, police, judiciary. See Bunyan, T., *The History and Practice of the
      Political Police in Britain*, Appendix II (London: Quartet Books, 1976).

37   See for instance: *A Doctor Recalls the Newport Chartist Uprising*. South
      Wales Argus. 3/11/2017.

38   See for instance: The Battle of Orgreave during the 1985 miners' strike.

39   See for instance *The Guardian*, 4 Feb 2013. 'Lincoln's great debt to Manchester.'

40   History Ireland. https://www.historyireland.com/who-were-the-manchester-martyrs.

41   Cope, Zak (2015), *Divided World Divided Class*. For the continued effects of this on the British labour movement today, see Dan Glazebrook, *The Tragedy of Corbynism*. Couterpunch. 27/12/2020.

42   Cope (2015). Lenin, V.I., 1999. *Imperialism: The Highest Stage of Capitalism*. Resistance books.

43   Caroline Elkins. Imperial Reckoning. *The Untold Story of Britain's Gulag in Kenya*. (Owl Books, New York, 2003) pp. 9-12.

44   Elkins (2003) pp. 9-12.

45   Elkins (2003) pp. 12-30.

46   Elkins (2003) pp. 12-30.

47   Elkins (2003) pp. 12-30.

48   Elkins (2003) pp. 154-191.

49   Newsinger (2015) p. 70.

50   Elkins (2003) pp. 62-89. Newsinger British Counterinsurgency. (London. Palgrave Macmillan. 2015) pp. 80-81.

51   Elkins particularly pp. 62-89. Newsinger (2013) pp. 12. Ian Cobain. *Cruel Britannia, A Secret History of Torture*. pp. 78-90. Newsinger (2015) p. 81.

52   Cobain (2015) p. 80. Elkins (2003) pp. 48-49. Newsinger (2015) p. 81.

53   Elkins (2003) pp. 62-89.

54   Elkins (2003) pp. 244-258.

55   Elkins (2003) p. 221.

56   Elkins. (2003) pp. 233-274.

57   Elkins. (2003) pp. 233-274.

58   Newsinger (2015) p. 33. See also, History Ireland. Issue 1 (January/February 2014), Volume 22. (https://www.historyireland.com/frank-kitson-northern-ireland-british-way-counterinsurgency).

59   Elkins. (2003) pp. 233-274.

60   Elkins. (2003) pp. 233-274.

61   Elkins. (2003) pp. 233-274.

62   Elkins. (2003) p. 89.

63   Elkins (2003) p. 222.

64   Elkins. (2003) pp. 192-232.

65   Elkins (2003) pp. 361-362. Newsinger (2015) p. 87.

66   Elkins. (2003) pp. 148 and 201.

67   Richard D Woolf. I hate to reference a podcast, but this one is exceptionally accessible while also being comprehensive and rare in that it analysises neo-colonialism from the economic perspective. Economic Update: The Economics of Colonialism Pt. 2 – The Neo-colonialism Variation. Podcast. 17/10/22.

68   See for example: *The Guardian*. 24 Oct 2013. *Economics Students Aim to Tear up Free-market Syllabus*.

69   Michael Hudson. *Killing the Host*. Plus: Nick Romeo. *Is It Time for a New Economics Curriculum?* The New Yorker, October 8, 2021.

70   For exhaustive detail: Claire Provost, Matt Kennard. Silent Coup. (Bloomsbury. London. 2023). The themes of the book are summarised very clearly and concisely in an interview here: 'Matt Kennard interviewed by Novara Media and exposes government, corporate and aid corruption.' Podcast, 30/6/23.

71   Provost, Kennard. (2023) Plus Matt Kennard interviewed by Novara Media and exposes government, corporate and aid corruption.

72   Provost, Kennard. (2023) Plus Matt Kennard interview. Podcast. 30/6/23.

73   Michael Hudson, *The Destiny of Civilisation*. (ISLET, London, 2022) p. 147.

74   Matt Kennard Interview. Podcast, 30/6/23.

75   Hudson. (2022). Hudson gives other examples of such legal cases including: Phillip Morris attacking Australia's cigarette labelling policy; European firms attacking Egypt's post-revolution minimum wage increase and South Africa's post-apartheid affirmative action law. p. 148.

76   Hudson. (2022). p. 147.

77   Provost, Kennard. (2023). p. 35. Plus Matt Kennard interview. Podcast. 30/6/23. Hudson (2022). p. 148.

78   Hudson (2022). p. 148. Matt Kennard Interview. Podcast. 30/6/23.

79   Provost, Kennard. (2023). p. 35. Plus Matt Kennard Interview. Podcast. 30/6/23.

80   Zac Cope. *The Wealth of (Some) Nations. Imperialism and the Mechanics of Value Transfer*. (London, Pluto Press. 2015).

81   Walter Rodney. *How Europe Underdeveloped Africa*. (Washington DC, Howard University Press, 1982).

82   For a massively detailed analysis of the economic mechanisms of exploitation and their meaning for the continued prosperity of the West – and how it splits the working-class movements of the global North, see Zak Cope's fabulous *The Wealth of (Some) Nations* (see note 87). But warning: you'll need a dictionary and a brain surgeon on hand in case of emergency.

83   Cope (2015) p. 43.

84   Kehinde Andrews. *The New Age of Empire: How Racism and Colonialism Still Rule the World*. (London: Penguin. 2021).

85   Andrews (2021).

86   First coined in relation to the Argentine dictatorship 1976-83. Also used to describe the British war in Ireland 1970-1992. See for example, *The Irish Times*, *Secrets and Lies: Britain's Dirty War in Ireland*. May 17 2018 https://www.irishtimes.com/culture/books/secrets-and-lies-britain-s-dirty-war-in-ireland-1.3498924. It's worth saying here that The Dirty War has recently been rebranded/restyled/further disguised in Britain as 'humanitarian intervention.' But the principle of secret Western war against the global South remains intact. See Yugoslavia, Iraq, Afghanistan Libya, Syria, etc. But this is a whole other essay. Or play. Or both.

87   Mark Curtis. *Secret Affairs: Britain's Collusion with Radical Islam*. (London. Serpent's Tail.) And, McCoy, A.W., 2003. *The Politics of Heroin: CIA Complicity in the Global Drug Trade, Afghanistan, Southeast Asia, Central America*. *Chicago*. IL: Lawrence Hill. For a detailed but still concise exploration of CIA and the global drug gangs, see the essay in my playscript, *The Political History of Smack and Crack*. (London, Nick Hern, 2018).

88   See for example. A Briefing by Mark Curtis and Nafeez Ahmed.The Manchester Bombing: Blowback from British state collusion with jihadists abroad. https://medium.com/insurge-intelligence/the-manchester-bombing-as-blowback-the-latest-evidence-83ec2127801d. Also: Alison Banville. MI5 was complicit in the activities of Manchester Bomber Salman Abadi. Morning Star. https://morningstaronline.co.uk/article/mi5-was-complicit-activities-manchester-bomber-salman-abedi.

89   Now named Western Hemisphere Institute for Security Cooperation, the place is still doing its dirty work today. (See: https://soaw.org/soa-watch-then-and-now).

90   See for instance: Livingstone, G. *The School of Latin America's Dictators*. *Guardian*, Fri 19 Nov 2010. (https://www.theguardian.com/commentisfree/cifamerica/2010/nov/18/us-military-usa).

91   Arditti, Rita. *Searching for Life: The Grandmothers of the Plaza de Mayo and the Disappeared Children of Argentina*. (Berkeley: Univ of California Press, 1999).

92   Frank Kitson. *Low Intensity Operations: Subversion, Insurgency and Peacekeeping*. (London: Faber & Faber, 2013).

93   Frank Kitson. *Gangs and Counter-gangs* (London: Barrie and Rockliff, 1960).

94   See History Ireland. *Frank Kitson in Northern Ireland and the 'British way' of counterinsurgency*. Issue 1 (January/February 2014), Volume 22. https://www.historyireland.com/frank-kitson-northern-ireland-british-way-counterinsurgency.

95   *See Brits Speak Out. British Soldiers Impressions of the Northern Ireland Conflict*. Compiled by Jon Lindsay. (1998). In the former soldiers reported that their official training on arrival in the north of Ireland was all about the peacekeeping mission – ie 'keeping Catholics and Protestants apart', while as soon as they began operations everyone understood they were there to fight the Irish Republican movement based in the poorest Catholic communities. One corporal expressed frustration that because their enemies in Ireland were white they could not 'go in hard' like they had in the colonies to finish the job.

96   Kitson was appointed head of the UK army in the wake of the 1981 inner-city uprisings in Birmingham, Brixton, Bristol, Liverpool, Leeds, Manchester, Tottenham. From there he went on to reorganise the whole security apparatus of the UK, especially the police force – but also for example the design of new housing estates to enable better response to potential future uprisings. He was appointed Aide-de-camp to Queen Elizabeth II after the scandals about his activities in Ireland had resulted in his removal from the Northern Ireland Command.

97   See for example: Conla Young. *IRA 'Gibraltar Three' Remembered 30 Years On. The Irish Times*, 6/3/2018. https://www.irishnews.com/news/northernirelandnews/2018/03/06/news/ira-gibraltar-three-remembered-30-years-on-1270659.

98   http://news.bbc.co.uk/onthisday/hi/dates/stories/march/16/newsid_2523000/2523953.stm.

99   Fredrick Engles. *A Polish Proclamation*, 11 June 1874.

A Nick Hern Book

England & Son first published in Great Britain as a paperback original in 2023 by Nick Hern Books Limited, The Glasshouse, 49a Goldhawk Road, London W12 8QP, in association with HOME and Tin Cat Entertainment

Cover image: Design by Greg

Designed and typeset by Nick Hern Books, London
Printed in Great Britain by Mimeo Ltd, Huntingdon, Cambridgeshire PE29 6XX

A CIP catalogue record for this book is available from the British Library

ISBN 978 1 83904 265 2

www.nickhernbooks.co.uk/environmental-policy

www.nickhernbooks.co.uk

 facebook.com/nickhernbooks

 twitter.com/nickhernbooks